DARK PSYCHOLOGY SECRETS

Discover the Winning Techniques of Emotional Manipulation - Influence People Through Mind Control, Persuasion, and Empathy. Defend Yourself From the Mind Games of Toxic People

Robert Covert

TABLE OF CONTENTS

INTRODUCTION

Murder, rape, incest, abuse, all words that can send chills up to your spine. As a culture, we have saturated ourselves with negative ideals for entertainment purposes. We sit and watch horror movies, crime shows, and reality shows diving into the minds of the deviant. The darkness within these becomes an obsession for some, and though they don't reenact or find the actions preferable, there is a connection that few want to outwardly recognize. While the majority of human beings have a buffer in their mind, knowing fact from fiction and right from wrong, some lack it.

Imagination is one thing. Combing through the worst fears of people to find what scenario can be the scariest and most grabbing is something that fiction writers and creators do. Often times though, when watching these dark psyches at work on the screen in front of you, the human mind finds a certain recognition of why the predator or villain did what they did. Some movies and books even prey on the idea of the worst human condition. Depraved and distraught, the father who witnessed his family's murders climbs out of his ominous depression to wreak havoc on those that committed the acts to begin with. There is a satisfaction for people in the revenge of heinous acts. But then, doesn't that apply the same dark psyche to the perpetrator, regardless of the reasoning behind it?

Dark Psychology has no pointed targets and cares little for the reasoning behind the actions. It is the actual act of manipulation, deceit, and harm that carries the weight within the dark psyche. The idea of revenge has been around a very long time, and at some significant points in history was considered a requirement of honor if the wrong was done to you. Very clear examples of the "eye for an eye" concept are still in existence today. The death penalty is one such example, though the root of it is wide and doesn't currently encourage the private actions of one person to another. The federal organization as a whole is in charge of carrying out the punishment. But long before that, laws were erected in civilizations that based themselves on the idea of revenge.

CHAPTER 1: WHAT IS DARK PSYCHOLOGY?

Most psychological techniques have a dual purpose – they can be used for both dark psychology and white psychology. What differs is the intent of the person employing the techniques.

In this chapter, we will concern ourselves with psychological techniques employed to achieve nefarious intents.

DARK PERSUASION

Persuasion is by far the most employed psychological technique. Most of the time, it is used for White psychology. As a tool for White psychology, almost all of us have used it in one way or another. However, very few of us have employed persuasion as a dark psychology tool.

Before we venture into the depth of Dark persuasion, let's look at the crucial components of persuasion as a whole.

WHAT IS PERSUASION?

Persuasion is a psychological technique of presenting arguments in such a way that motivates, influences, or changes a person's attitude, or behavior to achieve the desired outcome.

PERSUASION TIPS

The following are important tips you need to master to become successfully persuasive:

- Do your research – to gain knowledgeable authoritative

- Be a thought leader – to guide people in your thoughts

- Be confident

- Appeal to emotions

Use rhetoric statements and assertions

- Keep sarcasm to the minimum

- Sound reasonable

- Watch reactions

- Be subtle in responses

- Actively listen

- Suggest, don't demand

- Be actively observant

- Be emotionally intelligent

PERSUASION TACTICS

The following are basic yet important persuasion tactics:

- Use the name of the person you are engaging with

- Make a personal connection

- Build rapport

- Create an opportunity for reciprocity

- Use motivating words

- Be dynamic and adaptive – like a chameleon, change to suit your target's uniqueness (no blanket approach). Use NLP's mirroring and matching technique.

- Take advantage of the Bandwagon effect

- Create some scarcity in the mind of the person you are persuading

- Inspire curiosity through deliberate information gap (suspense)

- Use a foot in the door tactic – make a small request that opens the door wider for an eventual big request

- Clearly, point out the benefit of your proposition to the person you are persuading. Remember everyone subconsciously asks "what is in it for me?"

THE BANDWAGON EFFECT

Bandwagon effect refers to that effect a crowd or group of people has on its constituent member.

The following are some characteristic attributes of the bandwagon effect:

- The herd mentality – people are persuaded to follow each other

- Social proof - people tend to follow the most popular cause of action. For example, decrying negative social proof (such as littering, logging, bad sexual behavior, bingeing, smoking, etc) may promote it. For example, in case of 20% absenteeism, instead of the manager decrying that there is an increase of absenteeism from the previous 15% to now 20%, the manager should also reinforce positive social proof by pointing out to the majority who have remained not absent (i.e. 80%) and talk of the 20% as few spoilt apples that should be minimized.

DECEPTION

Deception refers consciously and deliberately promoting that which is not true with the aim of covering-up, misleading, or promoting a belief, concept or idea to manipulate the recipient to act or respond in a certain predetermined way.

In other words, deception is the manipulation of appearances such that they convey a false reality.

The core essence of deception is to disguise. Some of the common deception methods include:

- Propaganda – propagating false information and packaging it as truth or facts

- Camouflage – disguising the true nature of things. For example, a spy using philanthropy to penetrate a community.

- Pretension – taking a form that is false from the true form. For example pretending to be innocent while guilty, pretending to be sick while well, pretending to grief while inside you are celebrating, etc.

- Mystification – creating a supernatural sense by hoarding truth and acting in a way that appears supernormal. This makes you attractive to those who are prone to beliefs.

- Paltering – speak or act in such a manner that bamboozles people and as such draw their attention away from themselves and towards you. Eventually, you manipulate their attention towards achieving your own set goals. Conjurers, magicians, and actors employ this tactic.

TYPES OF DECEPTION

Deception occurs in two primary forms:

- Lie by commission (dissimulation) – this is the active part of the deception. In lie by the commission, a person deceives or lies directly by deliberately altering material facts.

- Lie by omission(simulation) – lie by omission is indirect. In this regard, a person engaged in deception does not deliberately alter material facts. Rather, the person knowingly and deliberately conceals material facts which he or she knows that would have altered the decision of the person being deceived.

DUPERY

Dupery is an act of deception. However, dupery goes further to selfishly gain from the victim. In dupery, the manipulator sets traps or baits into which the victim falls in and then gets exploited for selfish or nefarious gains.

INDOCTRINATION

Indoctrination is the act of imparting someone with a set of beliefs without offering that person an opportunity for critical inquiry.

INDOCTRINATION STRATEGIES

Rote training – this is an act of enforcing information into people's memory through repetitive action. For example, uttering certain mantra during prayers, or counting mala beads while praying.

Affirmation–making people say words that positively approve certain statements. This way, they are programmed to hold those statements as true.

Obstruction of truth and facts–this is a deliberate action aimed at making those being indoctrinated not to access sources of truth or facts. For example, they can be barred from reading certain books that are deemed "satanic". Fear psychology is often employed, like telling people that they will have nightmares or be visited by vampire spirits in their sleep if they read such a book.

Confession–everyone one of us has a "sinful" past. We all have skeletons in our past... things that we did and feel guilty about. One indoctrination strategy is to force people to confess. Once they confess, they lose the moral authority to stand upright before the indoctrinators. As such, they become more submissive toward indoctrination.

Isolation – the main aim of isolation is to cut out someone from the influence that may make indoctrination impossible or difficult to achieve. Thus, the victims are cut off from the rest of the family, society or normal relationships. Isolation is one form of obstruction of truth and facts since the victims cannot get a second opinion about assertions being made by the indoctrinators.

Guilt imposition – guilt imposition is closely related to forced confession. However, in guilt imposition, a sense of guilt is postulated into the victim's mind. The victim may be unknowingly ensnared to commit a wrong and then indoctrinator finds ways to discover it. Later on, the indoctrinator uses that act to impose guilt on the victim. The primary objective, just as forced confession, is to lower the victim's moral standing and hence cower the victim into psychological submission.

Phobia imposition – phobia is psychological fear. Indoctrinators induce phobia into their victims such that they find it hard to exist outside the indoctrinator's domain. For example, the victim can be told of how the 'devil' wants to kill him and the only way to salvation is to leave that devil-infested home and come to live with the indoctrinator who has the powers to chase away the devil. There are many forms of phobia imposition. For example, insurance companies impose phobia on their potential clients by exaggerating the potential risks that may happen should the potential client not insure the life of loved ones or property. Governments also prey on their citizens by instilling phobia, especially when they want their agenda to prevail.

Rituals – rituals have a strong effect on one's psychology. This is why most traditions, religions, cults, political organizations, and even some civil organizations have rituals. For example, it is common for rituals to be performed before prayers, burials, wars, etc. Rituals enhance a person's susceptibility to a certain proposition being advanced by the indoctrinator.

Induced dependency – induced dependency is commonly applied by manipulators in a relationship where they want to gain an upper hand over their victims. For example, imperialist or colonialist entities can perpetuate poverty in their target society and then pretend to be saviors of that society. They may dish out conditional aid, conditional grant, etc... with the conditions carefully crafted to increase dependency and make the victims more susceptible to exploitation. Since, without this deliberate impoverishment, that particular society would not have become susceptibly poor or would not have welcomed the conditional aid and grant, this becomes and induced dependency. In marriage partners, it is common for an insecure partner to create a condition that makes the other partner dependent. For example, an insecure husband can push or trigger his wife to lose employment. Once the wife loses employment, then, the insecure husband feels comfortably in control of the unemployed wife since he is the main breadwinner. The wife's lack of financial independence makes her become more susceptible to the dictates of the husband.

Punishment – by having a system of tests and exams and offering incentives for those who pass the indoctrination program

CHARACTERISTICS OF INDOCTRINATION

Unsurprisingly indoctrination takes place in most domains of our lives. It takes place in our homes (by parents), in schools (by teachers), in public life (by politicians and governments), etc.

The following are some of the key characteristics of tools used for indoctrination:

- Fear

- Dogmatism

- Fundamentalism

- Cognitive closure

- Feeling of inadequacy

- Perceived deprivation

SOURCES OF INDOCTRINATION

While there are some covert sources of indoctrination, the following are some of the common overt sources of indoctrination:

- Religious institutions

- Schools and educational establishments

- Media – mainstream, alternative media, social media

- Parents

- Politicians

- Marriage partners

BRAINWASHING

Brainwashing refers to erasing from one's belief system the existing set of old beliefs and in its place supplanting a new set of beliefs. Brainwashing happens without someone's will.

While sometimes brainwashing is subtle and involuntary, a lot of time it is violent. For example, we've had forced conversions during the crusade period and also during the jihad. In the forced conversion, the victims are fully aware that they are being brainwashed but accept it as a coping mechanism to avoid greater harm such as death.

Violent brainwashing happens most in the militant cultic or criminal organizations where victims are trapped and have no exit option.

Potential victims of violent brainwashing include:

- Prisoners (especially prisoners of war)

- Slaves under captivity

- Kidnapped victims

- Illegal aliens

In the subtle brainwashing, often the victim voluntarily and unknowingly accepts brainwashing. In this case, the perpetrator looks out for susceptible victims who are more malleable. The victims are often in a desperate situation and thus have a psychological void that desires fulfillment.

- The following are some of the potential victims of unknowing brainwashing:

- Those suffering from unknown chronic illness

- Minors who have left their home to live alone and
  often faraway

- Those who have lost their jobs and are in deep
  despair

- Those who have lost their loved ones, especially
  through divorce or death

COMMON STEPS IN BRAINWASHING

The following are some of the common steps taken by
brainwashers to brainwash their victims:

- Isolation

- Attack on self-esteem

- subjugation

- Testing

- Love bombing

ISOLATION

The brainwasher knows that a person's family or close circle can easily notice what is happening and thus rescue the victim. As such, the first step they take is to isolate the victim from close family and friends.

Some, like cultic leaders, can instill negativities about close family and friends. This brings division between the victim and loved ones and thus breeds psychological isolation. For example, a cultic leader can claim that your closest friend is a psychic vampire that drains your energy thus making you chronically ill and as such you ought to keep off from that friend. Since you are sick and desperate, you are likely to follow this brainwashing tactic and thus find yourself isolated from the very person who could have saved you from brainwashing.

ATTACK ON SELF-ESTEEM

It is only a victim who has self-doubt, low self-confidence, and on the overall suffers from low self-esteem that can easily be brainwashed. As such, the brainwasher seeks to achieve this state in the victim by attacking the victim's self-esteem.

Some of the ways by which the brainwasher attacks the victim's self-esteem include:

- Verbal and physical abuse – this often applied in violent brainwashing where the brainwasher uses abuse as a means of demeaning the victim so that the victim loses self-worth.

- Sleep deprivation – a sleep-deprived person is more likely to submit to psychological pressure since there is a lack of full consciousness. It is much easier for a sleep-deprived person to submit to brainwashing instructions just to have an opportunity to be left alone and sleep.

- Intimidation–Intimidation is one of the tactics employed by brainwashers to push someone into involuntary submission. For example, the threat of punishment is a form of intimidation.

- Embarrassment – this is used especially if the victim has some dark secret that he or she wouldn't like to be revealed. For example, a brainwasher may resort to using tricks to obtain nude photos of a potential victim or trick such a victim into marital infidelity. Once the brainwasher acquires these materials, he/she starts subtly embarrassing the victim. In this subtle embarrassment, the brainwasher doesn't reveal the materials to the public but uses generalized terms that insinuate immorality on the part of the victim. The victim knows where the cues are leading to and thus does everything possible to dissuade the brainwasher from revealing these embarrassing contents. Thus, the brainwasher attains an upper hand which he/she uses to brainwash the victim. For example, the victim could be forced into performing rituals that wear the victim's self-worth and self-esteem thus becoming deeply captive to the brainwasher. Eventually, the victim may be infected by the Stockholm syndrome, where, instead of acting against the brainwasher, acts to protect the brainwasher – an act, which, subconsciously is more about protecting the "secrets" (embarrassing content).

- Scarcity creation such as rationing of basic necessities and only released upon the victim's obedient performance.

SUBJUGATION

Brainwashers seek to bring the victim under their absolute control so that the victims become absolutely obedient.

The following are some of the tactics used to achieve subjugation:

- Extreme abuse

- Us -vs- Them

- Love bombing

EXTREME ABUSE

The victim is passed through extreme abuse. Almost often emotional and psychological abuses are employed. Physical abuse is only employed in violent brainwashing. Physical abuse is not employed in the subtle brainwashing.

US -VS- THEM

The victim is coerced to make a choice between the brainwasher and the rest of the world. However, the victim is not granted an exit option.

The victim is introduced to those who are already brainwashed and thus praise the brainwasher. In case the victim still thinks of "them" (the outside world) as an option, the victim continues to be subjected to extreme abuse until he or she comes the ultimate choice of belonging to "us", that is, joining the rest of the brainwashed subjects.

TESTING

Testing happens to establish whether the victim has ultimately made the "us' choice and no longer desires to join "them". It is also done to test the victim's level of obedience.

Sometimes, under secret control, the victim may be released to "them" (the rest of the world) on the condition that he or she should return on a certain date. The victim is then secretly monitored to see whether he/she desires to return to "us" (the brainwashed group).

If the victim doesn't desire to return to "us", then, the victim is kidnapped and returned to the fold upon which the vicious cycle begins.

On the other hand, if the victim voluntarily returns to us, then, the victim is taken to the next stage, that is, love bombing.

More often than not, due to isolation and induced dependency, even if the victim desires to rejoin "them", the victim finds it such a long journey to recovery and hence prefers getting back to "us" rather than starting all over again to rebuild the lost life.

LOVE BOMBING

Once tests are done and prove that the victim has been effectively brainwashed, love bombing is applied to galvanize the victim into the fold.

Love bombing could be in the form of praising, promotion in the order of subjects, receiving gifts, etc.

DARK SEDUCTION

Dark seduction refers to the use of dark psychological tools to entice someone into engaging in a relationship that satisfies seducer's self-interest with no apparent benefit to the seducee.

A dark seducer orchestrates the victim's longings to suit his/her selfish desires.

While seduction is traditionally related to the opposite sex, it can also be of the same gender and asexual.

Dark seduction is not necessarily about sex but taking advantage of sexual arousal to achieve certain objectives.

When a victim is sexually aroused, the victim becomes less logical and less rational and thus more susceptible to manipulation.

The following are some of the dark seduction techniques:

- *Love bombing*

- *erotic expressions*

- *platitudes*

- *gifting*

- *sexual innuendos*

The primary objective of dark seduction is to appeal to the primitive Id within every individual and reduce the effect of anti-cathexis. This makes the victim break away from super-ego and hence lowers to the primitive level of Id where hedonism is prevalent.

Erotic actions and rewards are applied to the victim to reinforce this state of Id and completely wear off the super-ego and anti-cathexis.

More often than not, indoctrination and brainwashing can be applied to facilitate the wearing off of the super-ego.

HYPNOTIZATION

Hypnotization is the act of drawing a person's mind to a receptively vulnerable state that is irresistibly open to your suggestions.

A hypnotized person is like a sleep-walker whose consciousness is deeply focused on the act of walking and completely isolated to signals emanating from the rest of the environment.

While in that state of hypnotism, the hypnotized person cannot consciously draw references from external sources but only from the suggestions. The person either largely or completely loses peripheral awareness. Thus, the person's mind is trapped into some sort of a conscious bubble that is impermeable to intrusive signals from the rest of the awareness.

HYPNOTIC INDUCTION

Hypnotic induction refers to employing a series of preliminary instructions and suggestions to draw someone into hypnosis.

Key features of hypnosis:

Concentrated attention to a single object or idea

Isolation from peripheral awareness

Increased reception to suggestions

DARK VS WHITE HYPNOSIS

The difference between white and dark hypnosis rests in the intent of the hypnotist. Dark hypnosis is intended to exploit the hypnotic person for selfish gains by the hypnotist.

White hypnosis is intended to improve the condition of the hypnotic by helping the hypnotic snap out from a traumatic or harmful state of consciousness.

Hypnotherapy is the most common type of white hypnosis. White hypnosis is often referred to as therapeutic hypnosis.

HYPNOTHERAPY

Hypnotherapy is a form of white hypnotic induction practiced by medical practitioners for therapeutic purposes. The main aim is to help a patient heal from psychological, emotional, emotional, and even physical trauma.

Hypnotherapy can be used in pain relief in such a manner that enables the patient to dissociate himself from the source of the pain thus lessening sensitivity to that pain.

Facts about hypnosis:

- It is voluntary

- It is willful

- Children are more susceptible to hypnotism than adults

- 15% of people are highly susceptible to hypnotism

- 10% of people can hardly be hypnotized

- Those people who are easily absorbed in fantasies are more susceptible to hypnotism

Negative effects of Dark hypnotic induction

There are many victims of dark hypnotic induction. The following are some of the common causes of dark hypnotic induction:

- *Being hypnotized to such an extent that you willfully give your possession to the hypnotist*

- *Being hypnotized such that you willfully open your door to robbers*

- *Being hypnotized such that you voluntarily follow kidnappers to their den*

Psychological manipulation

Psychological manipulation is the act of employing deceptive, abusive or underhanded tactics to change a person's perception or behavior.

THE CODE OF HAMMURABI

The Code of Hammurabi dates back to Babylonian times. Around 1760 B.C., the king of Babylon set forth a stone pillar inscribed with the laws of his kingdom. They are considered to be the oldest discovered set of laws in our history as human beings. What is so significant about the Code of Hammurabi? It is the fact that it is set in the pure idea of revenge. King Hammurabi believed wholeheartedly in the idea of an eye for an eye and set forth over thirty laws of Babylonia based on that specific theory.

Through time, this code has shown its influence through almost all judicial and legal systems. Even the American justice system is predicated on the idea of an eye for an eye. A punishment system where retribution for a crime is equal in severity to the crime committed. What was not expected or understood was the fact that this revenge system is actually, internally governed by a specific part of our brains called the dorsal striatum. This sector controls the idea of revenge within our minds. For victims of crime, the dorsal striatum is more active. So ultimately, with a society of an eye for an eye, we are taking the actions of a dark psyche and melding a new one from their actions.

One very prominent case of revenge on a large scale would be the St. Bartholomew's Day Massacre. This massacre occurred during the Protestant Reformation in the sixteenth century. During this time, a new sect of Christianity had been created, and the Catholic Church stood to lose control and power over people, land, and money. In the August of 1572, the French Protestants flooded Paris for the marriage of a Catholic woman to a Protestant aristocrat. When the wedding was over, King Charles IX, ordered that the aristocrat be killed for his crimes to the church. In order to make it as easy as possible, he also ordered the murder of the Protestants within the town and then outward into the French countryside. That case of revenge cost society between a thousand and four thousand lives.

Let's take a look at the current day defining qualities of Dark Psychology.

CHAPTER 2: TECHNIQUES OF DARK PSYCHOLOGY

Now that you have a suitable baseline for understanding dark psychology's nature and practice, remembering that practice is at the core of dark psychology's nature, that it exists to be *used* more than studied, you are ready to start learning about the tools employed by dark psychology practitioners the world over. You will additionally remember that, while the terms "tools," "techniques," and "methods" will be used interchangeably throughout, it is best to think of these sub-crafts of dark psychology as first and foremost *tool*s, because tools, again, are objects meant to be *used*. If it helps, imagine dark psychology as a kind of carpentry, wherein you use these tools to build something. In the case of dark psychology, instead of a house or a table, that something the dark psychology practitioner is building is a subservient or otherwise personally beneficial social relationship-based like a house is based on a concrete foundation, on his or her target's (manipulated) desires.

MANIPULATION

In many ways, beyond containing within its deception, manipulation hints at and implies the existence of the other tools of dark psychology. In many ways, dark psychology is ultimately a *method* for better manipulation.

If you google "dark psychology" and click through the first few articles, you will see immediately that almost every source on dark psychology uses manipulation several to many times, and that in most cases it is a subheading within the article, or even in the subtitle to the article itself! This illustrates how significant manipulation is too dark psychology and how broadly the two are connected. In fact, as was hinted at above, manipulation could itself be split into several subcategories. Obviously, one would be *deception*, which was already covered. Otherwise, their *Machiavellianism, reverse psychology, semantics,* all of which could be described to some extent or another as kinds of *covert-aggression.*

All forms of manipulation could be described as covert-aggression because manipulation is inherently an aggressive social tactic. The proof of this is in the word "aggression" itself. Forms of aggression are, at their core, about exerting power over another person or animal. If a driver shouts aggressively at another car to "MOVE!" or because that driver of that other car cut him or her off, that driver is aggressive because he or she wants his or her will to take precedence over the other driver's will. He or she shouts "MOVE!" because he or she wants the other driver to move, in other words, and manipulation functions the same way. Unlike other forms of aggression, though, it has a secondary aim: avoid the detection.

This also speaks to the dark or sinister core of manipulation; it is always about power, and power is always, on some levels, angry and forceful. This is as true for semantic manipulation, a technique that can seem not just easy-going but even agreeable, as it is for Machiavellianism, a worldview named for a famously cynical and power-hungry author and politician.

To slow it down so as not to miss anything, we will unpack the concept of semantic manipulation. Chances are, you have experienced this method of manipulation in your life several times. It is, stated simply when a person insists that he or she understands words to mean something other than what they normally mean as a means of re-framing and controlling social interactions. Say, for example, a couple has a conversation where one, a man, tells his partner, a woman, that he really doesn't think very highly of her mother. Perhaps this was already an attempt at dark persuasion, which is coming up next, but perhaps not. Either way, the woman, understandably, gets upset with him for saying such a cruel thing out of nowhere. His response to her anger, however, disarms her immediately. He, calmly, tells her he didn't mean it negatively. "Thinking highly," he explains, means to him thinking that a person is imposing and scary. By "not thinking highly" of her mother, he meant that he saw her as a friendly and welcoming person with whom he could speak openly. In response, if he is successful, his partner becomes immediately less angry, believing herself to have misinterpreted his words. You can see how this can be useful on a basic level but also consider how, applied repeatedly, it creates a pattern wherein the practitioner is free from all criticism and looked at as a flawless, golden kind of person.

This desire, to be viewed as flawless or golden, is ultimately about getting others to put all of their trust into you, which could be considered an attribute common to a

Machiavellian worldview. As was said above, Machiavellianism's namesake was a famously cynical politician and writer. He is famous for writing the cynical statecraft how-to guide *The Prince*, a book where he breaks down the necessity of building loyalty by being seen to be perfect, and he coined the phrase, "The ends justify the means." This phrase gets at the core of the logic manipulation employs to function. Ultimately, manipulation is about using social tactics (means) cynically and knowingly, no matter how underhanded, to improve your social station (ends).

As you can see, deception is all-over the above methods. It is fundamental to most practices of manipulation. However it is important to note, that deception is *not* synonymous with telling lies. In fact, telling lies is just one subcategory of deception, which contains all manners of withholding, skewing or twisting of the truth *along with* the outright telling of falsehoods. This distinction is important because in many instances telling lies is nor the most efficient neither the most useful form of deception. Lies are often easier to detect and harder to pass-off than forms of deception that meld the truth with lies, or that function only as an absence of truth.

You probably have a passing understanding of reverse psychology, namely that it is telling a person to do one thing, so they do another. Well, it does run deeper than that, which seems to imply that people make decisions on a binary. This is not the case normally. One of the most brilliant things about reverse psychology is that, when deployed correctly, it is, itself, the impetus for limiting another's thought to a "yes or no" question. Say a skilled dark psychology practitioner decides he or she wants his or her friend to come along to the beach, but he or she knows that that friend hates going outside. In order to make that friend come along, he or she says, as if a normal statement, "You probably don't want to go. You're not really into *fun* like that." In that scenario, the dark psychologist is using reverse psychology, clearly, but what he or she is also doing is turning the question of whether or not to go to the beach into a question of whether or not that friend is fun. So, of course, the friend decides to go to the beach!

Hopefully, you're starting to get a picture of the varieties and permutations of manipulation as they function on people in the world. From the above, you should also get the idea that, while there are distinct words for different kinds of manipulation, ultimately they blend together and can be used in tandem with one another. There is no reason why an attempt at semantic manipulation can't be employed along with reverse psychology, perhaps as a means of framing the yes/no dichotomy through which the target of the manipulation is meant to think. Likewise, it is impossible to imagine Machiavellianism without covert-aggression, and fairly difficult to imagine the reverse. That is all to say that manipulation is ultimately a fluid thing, as you will see with the rest of the tools laid out in this chapter and, admittedly, with most ideas you engage with every day. Although these things are "dark," they function like anything else. Taken in reality, in their actual *use*, these concepts all blend together.

PERSUASION

A note before diving into the skillset known as persuasion – persuasion, in fact, exists in two varieties. There is, on the one hand, regular everyday persuasiveness. This is the persuasion people are talking about when they, for instance, reference persuasive writing techniques. It can also contain the social pressure of the ethically or morally-minded variety. On the other hand, though, and more in line with the topic of this book, is *dark persuasion*. This is the kind of persuasion that has more to do with personal gain than ethics or morality, the kind of persuasion that has no scruples about negatively affecting people's lives. It is the persuasiveness of con men, corrupt politicians, and amoral attorneys. All groups of people who are, you guessed it, routinely practitioners of dark psychology.

As was said above, manipulation can be viewed in a sense as a partial umbrella term for all of dark psychology. This *is* true, but in another sense, dark persuasion can itself be viewed as an umbrella term for all of dark psychology, which would mean that manipulation is itself contained in *it.* How, you ask, can manipulation and persuasion both contain each other? The answer, of course, is that categorizations are contingent and incomplete things a lot of the time. This ambiguity, however, is productive for the practitioner of dark psychology. Think back to the introduction, where the link between the power of the world and dark psychology was laid out. You will recall that knowledge of dark psychology has remained for elite eyes only – that is to say, obscured to your average person – for most of its history. Well, this ambiguity or confusion surrounding terms speaks to that secret history, where practice and not scholarly taxonomies or categorizations determined the shape of the world of dark psychology. Because it is shaped like this now, it is important to not smooth over the complexities it presents too much, lest you miss out on fully grasping, and perhaps taking part in, dark psychology.

That being said, look at dark persuasion and ask yourself how it could *differ* from manipulation. To start, persuasion, even of the dark variety, is much less aggressive than manipulation. This is not to say that it is wholly nonaggressive, because, as was said before, dark psychology is an inherently aggressive style of engaging with the social world. However, dark persuasion's aggressiveness is by and large, more deeply concealed than manipulation's aggressiveness.

This is because of a simple, but also fundamental, the difference in tactic. Persuasion could be considered a better first step in trying to bend the will of another person than manipulation, because it is more subtle, and even in the unlikely event of detection it can be passed off as socially acceptable behavior.

How does dark persuasion work, though? In order to answer that, first, look at the fundamentals of dark psychology. What is it? It is an intensely intimate method of control predicated on the subconscious of another person. With manipulation, there are shortcuts to accessing the subconscious of another person based on the basic nature of the human psyche. People are generally, even overwhelmingly, susceptible to at least some methods of manipulation, and those methods work even if you know very little about the person on which you are trying to use them. This is not so with dark persuasion. Dark persuasion, instead, is predicated on a certain kind of dark intimacy with your target. You have to know and understand his or her drives, interests, and dislikes. The more you know, the more effective the persuasion of your subject will be. In dark persuasion, unlike in manipulation, the dark psychology practitioner comes to understand the mind of the target in an old-fashioned way, by way of study, observation, and time spent around the target.

Note the term *dark intimacy* used above. It will come back later. For the time being, however, it warrants some unpacking. How, exactly, does dark intimacy differ from regular intimacy? The answer, as always, lies in intent. For the average person, intimacy is an end in itself. When the average person is emotionally intimate with another person, he or she feels seen, heard, appreciated, and generally good. Emotional intimacy is the bedrock upon which normal relationships, be they platonic, romantic, sexual, or familial, are based. None of this is the case in the dark psychology worldview, though. When you practice dark psychology, social relationships, no matter their type, are never an end in and of themselves. They are always a *means* to an end. It is a necessary component of the dark psychology methodology of control.

Therefore, intimacy in the context of dark psychology, what you would call dark intimacy, could not be further from its normal, not dark counterpart. It can take many forms. Dark intimacy may be based solely on the study of its target's inner workings. From Freud, we have the insight that, with enough observation and study, the subconscious of any person can become legible to others. Freud didn't have control of the other in mind, but the principle remains the same. That is to say; dark intimacy does not necessarily imply a real relationship of any kind. That being said, it can. Another form of dark intimacy, darker still than that dark clinical intimacy, is dark intimacy developed the old-fashioned way. It comes from entering into a relationship with another person and feigning normalcy, pretending that you are in the relationship for all the normal reasons, while secretly maintaining that relationship for self-interested, anti-social ends. This is a very potent set up for practicing dark persuasion. Only after you have established what the other person perceives as real, mutual trust will you be able to enact your dark persuasion, but it will be very effective. Once you understand the target of your dark persuasion inside and out by way of dark intimacy, you can begin.

You already know the importance of deception to all practices of dark psychology. It comes out in full force here, because what underpins the differences between dark and regular persuasion is that, unlike regular persuasion, dark persuasion has no fidelity to the truth or the world. It has fidelity only to success in persuading its target and to the whims and wishes of the person deploying it. So, once you, the dark psychology practitioner, have developed a suitably intimate, which is to say *close*, understanding of your target, such that you understand as many of his or her wishes, insecurities, drives, and desires as you can, you deploy persuasion techniques as needed without any heed to the truth. If your target wants to be beautiful, and you want your target to make a large purchase on your behalf, for instance, you may be able to find a way to convince him or her that he or she will be more physically attracted to you if he or she *makes* that purchase for you. When you are practicing dark persuasion, it does not matter if this could not be further from the truth. Even if you knew that never in a million years, would you find that target physically attractive?

These are the fundamental attributes of persuasion, or, more specifically, dark persuasion. The detour into dark intimacy was necessary, because without dark intimacy of some kind or another dark persuasion simply can not work. Unlike manipulation, which has a higher success rate on strangers, dark persuasion must be predicated on some knowledge of the target's inner workings, or at the very least in-depth knowledge of how and what most people desire.

CHAPTER 3: DECEPTION- BEYOND THE LITTLE WHITE LIE

Everyone's done it. Small children don't know who made the mess or broke the lamp. The check is in the mail. We'll be ready in five minutes. Yes, you look wonderful in that dress. The little white lie. It's inherent in human nature. Before we look at how we can use lies and deception, let's look at why we lie.

LIES!

If humans are hardwired to lie, why? Where does the instinct to tell an untruth to come from? Is it biological or psychological, or both? The answer is both! Humans lie because of what scientists call a 'tend and defend' response. This means that lies are used to tend to needs or to defend against the threat, and there is a correlation between lying and the release of the brain chemical oxytocin, one of our innate 'feel good' hormones. When we have elevated levels of oxytocin, we are more likely to lie to avoid losing that feeling of a natural high.

There are several documented reasons for lying, which fall into either the tend or defend category. They are as follows:

1- Defend oneself- these are lies made to avoid punishment or backlash for action or perceived action;

2- Defend others- these are lies made to avoid others being punished or attacked for their actions or perceived actions;

3- Tend to oneself- these are lies told to gain control of a situation or a person, lies told to avoid embarrassment or awkward social situations, or lies told to gain personal desires or win admiration; and

4- Tend to others- lies told to protect others' secrets, to build other people up into greater figures than they are, and to maintain social facades.

Lies don't have to be earth-shattering, but when they become too big, it often becomes extremely difficult to keep a story straight. They say the best lies have an element of truth, and that seems to be the case. Lies often have harsh consequences when they are discovered, so if you are going to be deceptive, be sure to be emotionally prepared to deal with any fallout.

The fallout from Pinocchio's lies manifested physically as a growing nose!

WHEN DO LIES BECOME DECEPTION?

If you stop to think about lies, you'll realize that they almost have a scale. A little white lie about not having a babysitter might get you out of going to a party, so that's pretty low on the scale. But if you lie about not having a babysitter, but you don't need one because you are lying about having a baby, now that's a bit of a whopper. So where is the line?

Small lies, or fibs, often don't have many consequences. But larger lies, especially those that become compounded by repetition or addition, lead to a cycle of lying that eventually becomes destructive to self, others, or self. That cycle is most likely the definitive line between a lie and a deception.

Deception comes in many forms- lying about work or life experience, lying about the state of your relationships, lies of omission, and even lies which are told so many times, the liar themselves believe them. If lies can cause so much psychological damage, why do people still insist on using them?

HOW LIES APPLY IN REAL LIFE

It goes back to that 'tend or defend' response. Let's take a more in-depth look at why people could use lies for those purposes. The first reason on the list was to 'defend oneself'. Self-preservation is a powerful thing. If you are in an abusive relationship, you might lie about where you've been to avoid being verbally or physically attacked, even if your location would be somewhere perfectly harmless in a healthy relationship. If your abuser thinks you were at the grocery store rather than having coffee with a friend, you've lied to protect yourself from abuse.

The second reason was to defend others. This may follow closely a scenario like above, but perhaps it's a mother lying to protect her children from a physically or emotionally abusive authority figure. Another scenario might be an older sibling taking the blame for misbehaving when it was really the younger sibling that caused a mess or broke something valuable. Friends or coworkers may lie to stick up for each other in situations that they might otherwise get in trouble for.

The next item on the list about why people lie is to tend to themselves. There are many selfish reasons to lie, and it's probably the most common reason as well. People lie to take care of their own needs and desires, to get what they want from others. People lie because they want other people to like them, and so they exaggerate personal accomplishments and achievements to make themselves look better. We hear of this in cases of a transcript or resume fraud.

Lies that people tell to tend to themselves also frequently are told, no maliciously, but with the intent of covering up an embarrassing situation or avoid an awkward social interaction. These lies might be to hide a slip-up or to skip a party you don't want to attend. While these are little white lies, you may still face a little backlash when your husband's annoying cousin finds out you weren't really too ill to attend her bridal shower two hours away.

The last category of lie is the one that people tell to tend to others. This can mean being deceptive about liking someone's new haircut or lying about how good someone is at their job to help them get a good reference. Lies that we tell to tend to others tend to be lies of a positive nature, but that doesn't mean that they won't be susceptible to the same negative impacts as the other types of lies.

FAMOUS INSTANCES OF DECEPTION

Deception is one of the most ubiquitous methods are dark psychology. We see deception used in almost every era of human history. The Trojan Horse is a fabulous example of the power of trickery and deceit. A whole population believed they were receiving a gift, and instead, ended up with a massacre.

In the modern age, one of the largest stories to come out of a basis of deception is the rise and fall of Elizabeth Holmes and her health technology business Theranos. Holmes claimed to have invented a blood testing machine that could run full diagnoses with a minute amount of blood, primarily through a finger-stick. Holmes had her investors and board of directors completely fooled, and these weren't some joes off the street.

Billionaire media mogul Rupert Murdoch, the Walton family of Walmart fame, and the DeVos family, founders of Amway, all fell prey to Holmes's deceptions as investors in her biotech firm. She even fooled many well-heeled and well-educated board members, including several former or future United States Presidential Cabinet members. Holmes's house of cards came tumbling down when it was revealed that her miraculous blood testing equipment was deeply flawed and may have even risked the health of the people who'd relied on it. Before her lies being discovered, Holmes had managed to accumulate a net worth of $4.5 billion, all of which is gone today.

Holmes somehow hoodwinked some of the biggest scientific and entrepreneurial names in the country and all over the world. Now that's some serious deception!

THE ART OF CRAFTING A GOOD LIE

Telling a lie and selling a lie are two completely different things. Everyone knows when a preschooler is lying about who painted the living room wall. But when it's time to practice deception, how do you put together a story that's believable and watertight?

To tell an effective lie, it must be in part based on truth. It will be easier to remember, and you'll have a defense that you only bent the truth, not outright lied, should you get caught. You also should make your lie as simple as possible, to have fewer details to potentially mess up. If you have time to create your deception, practice telling it. It will come out much more naturally when it's time to tell it.

You shouldn't try to include anyone else in your lies-the more people who know what's happening, the greater chance of you getting caught. Lies and secrets are best kept to yourself. You should keep things brief and talk in your normal tone of voice when you deliver your lie. Make sure your body language and eye contact match your words and be sure that you could convince yourself of what you're trying to say.

Once you've told your lie, destroy any evidence. If you made a social media post, delete it. If you wrote something down, make sure you get rid of the piece of paper. Most importantly, don't compound your lie with another lie. If you get caught, it's probably best just to confess. Why? Because if you come clean and are honest, you're less likely to get caught the next time.

PANTS ON FIRE

Wouldn't it be wonderful if you could catch someone in a lie because their pants went up in flames? Unfortunately, liar, liar, pants on fire isn't a real phenomenon. There are ways to tell if someone is lying, no flames involved. Watch someone's eyes when they speak to you; if they seem unable to make eye contact or are very fidgety, they may not be being truthful with you.

Being able to spot a lie goes beyond fidgeting and shifty eyes, though. If someone has a delay in speech or a behavioral pause that they don't normally exhibit, they may be lying to you. Some experts say that a tell-tale sign of lying is if someone who doesn't normally touch their face or throat does so while speaking; likewise for playing with or running their fingers through their hair.

Speech signals could also denote when someone is lying to you. If someone repeats very simple questions before answering you, they could be buying time to craft a false response. You should also take note of any vagueness or lack of details when asked a direct question. If you suspect you're being lied to, ask the person to tell you their story again, but in reverse. The cognitive power it takes to remember a lie may make them slip up if they need to tell it out of order.

While there is no foolproof way to determine if someone is lying to you, use these tips and go with your gut, and you'll find that you'll improve your chances of ratting out a liar.

Don't discount your instincts, they can tell you more than

body language or speech patterns ever will.

CHAPTER 4: HYPNOSIS-FACTS, FICTION, AND THE PSYCHOLOGY THAT POWERS IT

Hypnosis is the subject of much skepticism, but the modern practices of hypnotherapy and the use of altered psychological states in the interrogation of prisoners would belie the number of raised eyebrows that hypnosis receives. The theory of hypnosis has its origins in ancient Egypt and India, where people were encouraged to heal themselves through spiritual journeys and altered states, and through 'temple sleep', a practice which encouraged people to rest in religious places to rejuvenate their minds and bodies.

In more modern times, hypnosis has taken on several different iterations, but they are all based on the theory that the mind can be controlled through a state of trance or altered state of consciousness. We're going to pick up the history of hypnosis shortly before it became popularized by Franz Mesmer.

HOW MESMER BEGAN MESMERIZING

When Franz Mesmer was a young medical student, he studied under a Jesuit monk named Father Maximillian Hell. Hell was an astronomer and researcher who was fascinated with the natural world and with the workings of the solar system, the polar regions of the earth, and the human body. Hell developed an interest in using magnets for the power of healing and introduced his student Mesmer to the technique of magnet therapy.

Mesmer took Hell's methods of magnet therapy, which involved using magnetized rocks to improve the flow of fluids through the body, and adapted and expanded their uses. Mesmer would often have patients swallow iron shavings, and then use a magnet to draw those shavings through the intestinal tract. Mesmer believed that people could be cured of what ailed them should he be able to get their 'vital fluid' back on track.

Mesmer called this early technique 'animal magnetism', and he truly was convinced that he could heal people through this magnetic laying on of hands. He later developed a technique which we more closely associate with hypnosis; this method involved sitting very closely with a patient while holding their hands and occasionally rubbing their shoulders, arms, and torsos while maintaining eye contact. After a while, the patients would convulse, and all their evil or poor feelings or illness would be relieved.

Skeptical yet? So were a lot of people at the time, and in 1784 a committee was formed to investigate not Mesmer himself, but one of his proteges, a doctor named d'Eslon, who had to perform Mesmer's treatments to mixed results. Why is all this important? Because the investigating committee discovered that the treatments were complete pseudoscience and that they were rooted in 'imagination'. But they worked, sometimes, so the real question is why?

ON TO THE NEXT THEORY

After Mesmer's works were largely downplayed and discounted, Mesmer himself retreated from medical practice, traveling Europe and living in relative obscurity until his death in 1815. A few decades later, Scottish surgeon James Braid would be the one to finally give some credence to Mesmer's practices.

Braid was a highly acclaimed physician and surgeon who pioneered a breakthrough way to treat clubfoot and other orthopedic issues of the extremities. In 1841, Braid was invited to a healing performance by one of Mesmer's former disciples, a Frenchman named Charles Lafontaine.

Lafontaine allowed doctors to come onto his stage while he was using magnetic treatments and examine his patients.

Braid was among the doctors to do so, and he observed that they all seemed to be in some sort of altered mental state. While Braid had been previously completely unconvinced that magnetism was a valid medical treatment, he was so intrigued he continued to attend Lafontaine's healing demonstrations until he could formulate a working theory as to why the treatments appeared to be successful. One thing he consistently observed was that the patients all seemed to be 'awake while sleeping'.

After some considerations, Braid concluded that the patients' altered states were a result not of Lafontaine's magnets, but his demeanor. The magnetist's behavior is what prompted the altered state, which Braid dubbed neuro-hypnosis, from the Greek for 'nervous sleep'. Braid began experimenting with the technique at home to see if he could induce the state by himself and deduced that a hypnotic state could be produced by visual or ocular fixation. This also completely debunked the use of magnets in Lafontaine's treatments.

Braid debuted his theory of hypnotism as a psycho-physiological phenomenon late in 1841, to mixed reviews from the scientific community. In his first lecture, Braid demonstrated that he could induce the same somnolent state as Lafontaine, but without the use of magnets. Although Braid had many opponents, who refused to believe that people could be healed through the power of suggestion, he would go on to integrate hypnotism into his medical practice as an alternative or complementary treatment for the relief of pain and other physical and psychological ailments.

THE POWER OF BELIEF

From the early origins of medical treatments using altered states to the modern hypnotherapies, we see used today, the underlying power of these methods is that the subject must *believe* that they work. A human brain is a marvelous machine, capable of higher thought and reasoning, and responsible for making sure our heartbeats and our lungs breathe.

But the brain is also a biochemical mass of electrical activity and multi-layered function. While we are usually in a state of full consciousness when we are awake, our brains are constantly working on a subconscious level, which usually manifests while we sleep. Hypnosis taps into a state of mind that is somewhere between waking and sleeping, but it does not work if the subject does not believe that it will. We've all seen performances where audience volunteers are put into a trance and asked to complete ridiculous tasks. There are movie tropes that center on a character behaving a certain way when triggered by a hypnotic keyword. How accurate are these portrayals?

CHAPTER 5: THE ROLE OF THE INTERNET IN DARK PSYCHOLOGY

It is an established fact that psychology is the scientific study that encompasses the study of human thoughts behavior emotions mind and so on. The beautiful thing is when one gets a deeper understanding of how psychology operates, it can be of great benefit not only to oneself but also in our everyday interactions with others. Man is a social being, therefore must process social behaviors which psychology seeks to understand, most time explains and sometimes predict.

Despite having many branches a large part of psychology is aimed at the diagnosis and treatment of mentally derailed individuals who possess a threat to the general public but depending on the perspective, Psychologists are versatile and cuts across many other areas. Also, note that psychology is all around you, your everyday activity, your interaction with others, that TV commercial you saw recently, the print ads, the website you are most frequent on and so on. All of these and more are either trying to persuade or convince you to bulge to whatever they are trying to offer.

Interestingly, there is psychology for any human problem no matter the age or gender which is why psychologist is bent on making life better and improving human behavior. As constructive, educative and informative as psychology maybe, there is a dark side to it. This aspect focuses on human consciousness as it relates to the nature of people prey on or victimizing others.

Dark psychology aims to understand the various thoughts, reasoning, perception or feelings that often lead to human predatory behavior because it entails the inhumane and brutal victimization of others without any reasonable human comprehension. Predators commit theft, abuse, and violence upon their victims and they appear in any form of personality. They are most times less compassionate and suspicious-looking.

Trolls generally can be annoying and irritating and can also be an agent of destruction/destruction. An internet troll starts quarrel and offends people on the internet. According to psychology, such people sometimes might have dark personality traits to them. They live such a life that is based on their sadistic nature and others must suffer the same fate and they naturally make you feel bad. Most times, there is a psychological disorder that is triggered by past experience or an ongoing occurrence, the best thing to do when you encounter one is to completely ignore them as they feed on your suffering which gives them great pleasure.

These internet trolls can be called a predator according to Michael Nuccitelli of predator.co. These people are first-class cyberbullies, stalkers, criminals, sexual predators, and the likes. These set of people use the power of the internet to gather useful information about their victims or targets.

A predator can be a group of people or persons that one way or the other, directly or indirectly enjoy stalking, exploring and victimizing unsuspecting individuals by using the power of information communication technology(ICT). They are most times consumed with their desire for power, imaginable fantasies or just suffering from loneliness and searching for acceptance. Age or gender is not a barrier as a predator can be of any age, gender or economic status. Initially, all we had was the human predator but with the rise of the technology age, things are now even more complicated as predators harness the power of ICT and use it to their advantage create profiles and stay almost untraceable.

- ### *Dark Traits And Online Activities*

The internet is a world on its own, it is a chain of network communicating with other billion networks out there as long as you are connected and the other party also, no matter where you are, you would definitely be connected. With the internet a whole lot can be done, you have access to almost anything you can think of. Information is just a click away once you stay connected and it has also made communication way easier. Despite having wonderful advantages, the disadvantages are life-threatening. One of the common disadvantages is that people work online 24/7 and spend a lot of time sitting while working in front of a computer often get ill. They get weaker, develop eye issues, back pain, and the likes. Some people get addicted, some fall into depression and isolation and others, serious health issues while many ends up with serious social issues or psychological disorder.

The internet often encourages the use of different behaviors and activities that have done offline to be practicalized online. Imagine someone addicted to sex, games or shopping, when such a person gets online, it becomes unlimited which later turns to a habit. If as a normal being, the internet has such an effect, imagine what it would pose in the hands of a predator. The Narcissism is proud and lacks empathy, the Machiavellianism is manipulative and lacks moral while the psychopathy is selfish and remorseless. Above all traits according to research has some things in common such as the lack of empathy.

Categorically, dark personality triad is a big influence in the behaviors of predators that trolls online. The online behavior of a Psychopathy can be a remorseless behavior while a Machiavellianism manipulates and Narcissism preoccupied with getting attention because of their self-behavior. All of these traits, one can easily use it to pinpoint an internet troll that possesses a dark personality. From several researchers, it was discovered that the personality triad behaviors are mostly found on social media platforms like Facebook and most trolls have a psychopathic tendency, unlike the Narcissist who promotes themselves or social status by the same social media platform.

The online activity of a Narcissist since he has pride would be a display of superiority by uploading images that shouts expensive, they can be materialistic and display a sense of superiority; they can be domineering and a thirst for power and Status. Machiavellianism on the other hand even though can have self-interest but theirs is to manipulate and deceive unknowing victims to achieve their own goals. The Psychopath in their own way is destructive of all the 3 personalities.

The Psychopath has no conscience, is violent in nature and very aggressive. The psychopathy is attracted to people that catch their attention either by social life or social status and so on. Hypothetically speaking, Psychopathic is most likely associated which trolling and_are more attracted to popular people on Facebook. Narcissism, on the other hand, might not be a troll but see themselves as being superior to everyone. They look down on people and they believe that they are special. Above all, Psychopathic traits can be sadistic and may find pleasure in harming others for fun's sake because they derive pleasure from it. So it is acceptable to say that abnormal online behavior is mostly Psychopathic traits.

- ***How The Internet Promotes Different Vices And Negative Traits***

The majority don't know that the internet is like an onion bulb consisting of different layers; we have the surface which is the aspect accessible to everyone, like your Google or Yahoo where we can buy things online or access our social media handles and the likes. Surprisingly, this surface web does not even make up for 10% of the internet we use, the remaining 90% is the real deal. They are what we call Deep Web and Darknet respectively. The deep web is only accessible to authorized persons as this is where private data such as legal documentation belonging to the government are stored. Also, medicals and academic information and not left out. The Deep Web is overseen by authorized and special services.

Moving deeper is the Darknet which is the most dangerous of them all, it uses the Onion Router (TOR). To have access, one would have to download the app. With just a click, one can end up in dangerous sites like the uncensored hidden wiki and many more. A site such as these provides information on drugs, weapons, pornography and so on. Various transactions can take place on the Darknet using our everyday services such as FedEx. An important thing to note is that users of the Darknet can be anonymous, every personal data can be concealed, secure and untraceable.

In regards to psychology, Psychologists have come to an understanding that there is a big relationship between the Dark personality traits which is the dark side of the human mind and the dark side of the internet. Some researchers even claimed that the amount of time spent online can increase or lead people to develop dark traits.

The question now is "is it the various online activities that attract individuals who already exhibit a good percentage of dark personality traits? Or can we say it is a long period spent on the internet that has increased these traits in individuals? There is a probability that both assumptions might be correct either way, the internet has over time become a sort for humans to explore their dark side. The internet has bred addicts because some negative traits seem to have been nurtured and encouraged by the internet which now possesses negative consequences when offline. The internet negative effect on personality is a functional part of online Psychology. With the help of the internet-related digital lifestyle, its effect on gambling or shopping is clear evidence of impulse control disorder.

Another negative trait is the rise of suicidal persons; it is no news that the suicide rate has risen over the years. One cannot commit suicide online but the increase of suicide definitely can be linked to an internet effect. The internet has also promoted online shaming, cyberbullying, name-calling and so on which is regarded as a violent online discourse which can lead to a less cohesive offline society. What about violent online games? Research has shown that offline aggressive traits can trigger exposure to violent games online.

The internet generally has psychological effects that once portrayed online, can remain relevant and be manifested offline even after one has logged off and these technologies are advancing as the day goes by. I asked how the internet has promoted or influenced the lives of people, the response definitely would differ as we have individual differences. The way of life nowadays can't be compared to the way people lived 20 years ago. These days we have fewer physical encounters and more of online interactions which in return creates a huge gap in humanity. Let us consider some disadvantages of the internet using social media as a case study;

- Reduction in emotional connection. In the days of old,if offended or you are the offender, you can easily talk it out with the other party, cry if you want to or perhaps punch some sense into one another and seal it off with a hug, case settled. in today's world with the rise of the internet or technology generally, if such should occur, one could send an 'I'm sorry' text and you wouldn't even know if the person is sorry or not. Using social media as a means of communication has killed our emotional connection one way or another. This is what some dark traits feed on you would never know what the other person is up to, all you see is an exchange of words until it gets too late.

- Avenue to hurt others. Remember the internet troll? They are the expert in this. They find pleasure in hurting others through hurtful words. It's a free world on the internet, you can say anything and get away with it. They forget that at the other end is a real person who has feelings and emotions but they can crush all that in just a line or two sentences. That is why some people end up timid or even commit suicide in extreme cases because of cyberbullying.

- Face-to-face interaction has gone. The way Mr. A would respond to you or communicate with you face-to-face can't be compared to how Mr will do the same if he is dependent on the keyboard. People now prefer to talk over a chart other than the old-fashioned meetup. No wonder a whole lot of Psychopaths are on the loose.

- Dead expression. You can be as angry as an erupting volcano but still, type LOL as a reply to a message. In the actual life, you are boiling with anger but laughing out loud via chat, who are we fooling? Laughter is an expression of a pleasant emotion and cannot be done otherwise but the internet has made it so.

- Lack of understanding. Because everyone is busy online, people tend not to understand other's feelings or emotions. Someone might be crying out for help but no one will be listening to why lack of understanding or perhaps thoughtfulness.

- Awkward interactions. Gaps have been created in so many relationships these days, friends and family now live as strangers; you are hanging out with friends or family and a single decent conversation could not be made because everyone is busy with his or her phone - someone is gaming online, another keeping up with the latest blog post or fashion trend or Sports update to mention but a few. There is a disconnection thus affecting relationships and creating this awkward feeling even when it's your loved ones.

- False self-image. This is the driving force of Narcissism, the average human lives a fake life on social media. We all tend to amplify our personalities to look cool and acceptable, your post must be perfect and flawless. You live in a world of imagination which you play online for others to see and admire. Sometimes, these displays cause others to feel bad about themselves only if they knew. Nobody wants to stay true to who they are and their identity, they cannot be blamed the Internet caused it.

- No family Bond. It's a family movie night, a time for the family to bond but Facebook, Twitter, texting or Instagram and the whole lot would not permit that to happen. We pretend to be watching the movie but in fact, we are not.

- Lack of attention. Findings have it that some accidents these days are caused by phone users, either the ones behind the steering or the ones walking by the roadside, why? Distractions here and there. The Internet can make one popular over time especially when you have a whole lot of friends and followers on social media platforms, you need to keep up with the trend so you spend most of your time online. This way you wouldn't take cognizance of things going on around you. Everything would suffer because of your lack of attention; your schoolwork, your businesses, friends and even families.

It is important to know that some people cannot imagine their lives without the internet and if you are among such people, then you might as well be a victim of the negative impact of the internet.

- Depression and anxiety because it promotes poor mental health which is a result of spending long hours online.

- Anxiety, the fear of missing out which is also a result of your frequent online activities; so you get anxious when you are not online because you feel a whole lot is happening and you are not a part of it.

- Body shame for someone who has no self-esteem such that would be thrown off balance by social media. If you don't value or love your shape, size, height or complexion, when you come on the internet you will encounter people who are better than you, the celebrities, wealthy people and the likes. These might have a negative effect on your body Image, never believe all you see some might just be a narcissist.

- Insomnia, it is no news that spending too much time online can create an unhealthy sleep pattern. It can make one lose quality sleep which in returns, effects general productivity.

Conclusively, the internet is more addictive than alcohol and the likes. Can you boast of a day you went without the internet or checking up on your social media handles? If Facebook decides to go off the radar today, would you be emotionally okay to bear it? We all are addicted one way or the other but the degree varies and it's on this note that the emergence of dark personality traits came to be.

- *Harmful avenues of Dark Personality*

Apart from the internet having disadvantages, it has also provided an avenue for people to lay their hands on harmful information about dark psychology thereby using it intentionally against one another. They should be searching for information as to identifying a manipulator or how not to fall victim instead people are after ways of hurting others or getting back at someone. They want to learn the art of dark personality traits and how they operate. Some of these harmful information is aimed at seeking to get an edge or more power in their everyday life. In the world of dark personality there are many faces to it, let us take a look at some of them;

1)You can manipulate another person's thoughts without the person's knowledge, this simple trick is called Covert Emotional Manipulation (CEM). With this act, you can hide your true nature and intention and the victim might have no idea until the dying minute which is always late the hour. In CEM, you can choose to focus on the aspect of emotions you want to manipulate which makes the process easier in some way. In a situation whereby the victim has a stronghold on his/her emotions, then the mission might be impossible.

CHAPTER 6: UNDETECTED MIND CONTROL

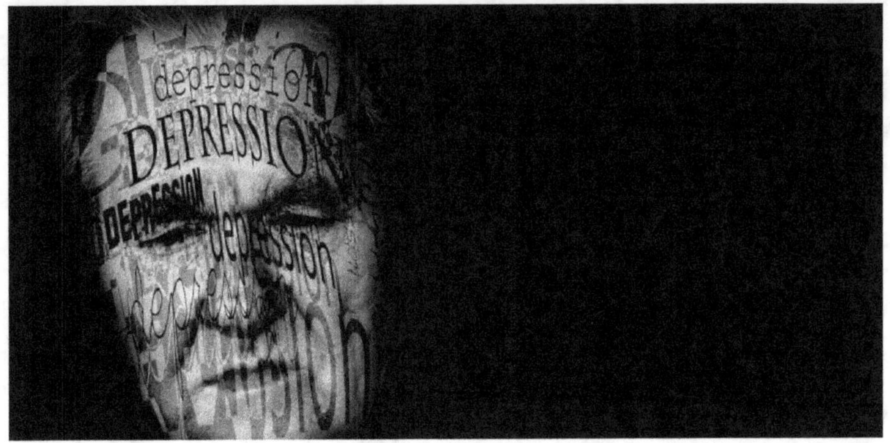

Your mind is your sanctuary. No matter what else can be lost to others, the mind is yours and yours alone. Or so we think. People like to believe that they are the ones in control of their own actions and thoughts. Many times, our minds can be susceptible to the influence of others, and this allows others to control our minds if we're not careful.

Think about a time when you watched a horror movie. Your mind and your emotions are already being led and influenced in the movie. All the decisions of the director, from the camera shot, the lighting, and the music can determine how you are going to feel and react. Even though you are in full awareness that you are just watching a movie, the brain is going to respond to the prompts when they are given. If our brain can be so influenced by something that we are aware of, how strong would the influence of a dark manipulator be?

Undetected mind control is often the deadliest type of mind control there is. If someone is already aware that their mind is being influenced, then they have the option to object, either physically, verbally, or mentally. For example, they can choose to avoid any contact with the person who controls them. A lot of people are going to run at the first sign they see a dangerous person trying to get inside the brain and take over. But if the mind controller can get into the brain of their victim without the victim detecting them, then the victim has no chance to put up their defenses before it's too late.

There are going to be two tactics that the manipulator can use to take over the mind of their victim without detection. This includes the use of media and interpersonal interactions. Traditionally, the media mind control was only possible for the larger company. Most individual mind controllers were left to deal with just the interpersonal interactions. But with the changes in technology now, this is no longer the case.

Smartphones and laptops have allowed even individual manipulators to have media mind control. This can make it a very powerful tool that the manipulator can use. While the undetected mind controller is going to be able to use all these methods, they are often going to be more deliberate and only take their actions after some careful consideration. They are sometimes seen as more coward compared to some other controllers, such as psychological manipulators, but they will take deliberate actions to find the right victim to attack.

UNDETECTED MIND CONTROL TACTICS

Now that we know a little bit more about undetected mind control, it is time to learn about some of the methods that are used by manipulators to control the mind of a victim in an undetected way. We are going to explore both the media and the interpersonal techniques that are in the toolkit of the manipulator. Let's take a look at some of the different undetected mind control tactics.

FINDING THOSE WHO ARE IN NEED

The first principle that comes with undetected mind control is to find a victim who has a goal. It has been proven that a person who has a pressing desire or needs is someone who will be more susceptible to this type of mind control compared to someone that feels satisfied and at ease. This could range from a small physical goal, such as someone who is thirsty and looking for a drink. Or it can be a more psychological goal, such as someone who is craving affection and love.

A good example of this is the experiment that was conducted to look at a subliminal influence or undetected mind control. In this study, there were two sets of people who were shown a film, but this film had a hidden image of iced tea. One set of people in the study were thirsty, and the second group wasn't.

After the movie, when the participants were given a chance to purchase a specific drink from a selection, the ones who were thirsty would purchase the iced tea in greater numbers compared to those who weren't thirsty. This shows that, when the brain is desperate for something, they are gladly taking suggestions on what they should choose.

So, how would you be able to use this principle with an individual on more of an interpersonal level? If the mind controller can find a victim who is already craving something in their life, then the manipulator will find that it is easier to control that victim. One example is a victim who just got out of a long-term relationship. They may crave the company again, and the mind controller would be able to influence their target into thinking that they are the savior for the victim. In reality, they are going to cause harm and even ruin for the victim, but the victim will crave attention so much that they will fall for the mind control that is put on them.

There are a lot of needs that a manipulator is going to seek to exploit their victim, including their need for company, their need to belong, and even monetary stability. These vulnerabilities are going to be exploited by someone who is more experienced for several purposes. They may want to financially or sexually exploit the victim. They may want to gain the victim's allegiance to form a cult or other extreme movement. Some manipulators just go through this process in order to toy with their chosen victims for their own pleasure.

RESTRICTING CHOICE

Restricting choice is another form of undetected mind control. It can be a subtle form of this because it is going to provide the manipulator with a range of built-in "get out clauses" if the victim ever starts to get suspicious. The key to this type of mind control is to take away any real choices that the victim has in a specific circumstance, while still providing the illusion that the victim is the one who has the control.

Let's say that there is a woman who is being asked to go out on a date. A regular guy is going to spend some time to ask the question and then stammer out an open-ended question. They may say something like, "Would you like to go out with me?" This question allows the woman to say yes or no based on their personal preferences. This is the way that people who aren't using manipulation will behave.

But someone who is trying to use mind control will approach all of this differently. They will confidently and smoothly work to charm the victim. They will get that person to laugh a bit and lower their guard. Then, with a lot of confidence and assurance, the manipulator will ask something like "So, am I taking you out on Thursday or Saturday?" This limits the choices that the victim can go with. The answer of no really isn't an option here, so the victim will pick one of the dates they are given. The victim can't really say that they weren't in control, but the manipulator had complete control the whole time.

Now, if the manipulator is caught or the victim realizes that they are limited in the choices they are allowed to make, the manipulator can backtrack and still look innocent. They could say something to their victim like "I can't believe you're analyzing my words so much. That really hurts me and makes me not want to open up to you." This can make the victim feel like they were mean, and they will likely give in.

MEDIA CONTROL WITH IMAGES

Just like our five senses can be guides in our lives, they can also be our enemies. Our sense of sight is very powerful. This is why we can even dream visually, even when all the other senses are missing, and we can use our sight to see images of memories. This can make imagery as well as visual manipulation a really powerful technique to use with media mind control.

Because of the changes in technology, impactful imagery techniques are in the hands of manipulators all over the place, and they can even take these techniques and tailor them to their specific victim. So, if their victim seems to have a fear or an aversion to something, the manipulator can use the feared images to help access and then warp the emotions of a person without the victim even realizing what's going on.

Let's look at how this type of mind control can work. We are in an age where there are lots of smartphones, videos, and more. Everything is shot in high definition clips and can be sent at fast speeds to someone else. This means that a high-tech manipulator can allude to the feared image. For example, if a manipulative boyfriend knows that his girlfriend has a big fear of insects, they could "accidentally" put a book with a picture of an insect on its cover in the background somewhere during that video chat. While the girlfriend may not consciously register that the book is there, on an emotional and subtle level, she is going to feel the impact.

MEDIA MIND CONTROL WITH SOUND

Sound is another method that the manipulator can use to do mind control. But personal experience and experiments can confirm this. Have you ever had a song that seems to get stuck in your head? How easy did you find it to get that song out of your head? The sound may have had a big influence over yourself, even though you knew it was there.

The power of audio manipulation is even greater when it is undetected. Experiments have shown that if customers are exposed to music that comes from a specific region, then they are more likely to order wine from that country. When they were questioned about it later, they had no idea that the sound around them was what influenced them for their decision making.

While there are examples with the media mind control with sound in the media and with the government, even individual manipulators can use this kind of mind control as well. One of the creepiest forms of this mind control is to subliminally influence the victim when they are asleep. A skilled mind controller can get their victim when that victim is at the most vulnerable, such as when they are sleeping, and then can implant the dark and devious commands in the ear of their victim. This allows the commands to sink into the lowest layers of the brain of that victim.

Another form of this auditory mind control is to mask the words with other words or noises that sound similar. Sounds that are outside the range of human perceptions can be this type of mind control. These sounds will reach a particular frequency, and they can be known to impart a feeling of unease, dread, or terror in those who are unknowingly exposed to them. Once the victim feels scared or trapped, the manipulator can then take control and do what they want from this point.

As you can see, there are a lot of different types of mind control that the manipulator is able to use on their victim. The one they choose will depend on the victim and what the end goal of the manipulator is at the time. The important part is that the manipulator needs to know their victim enough to do this type of mind control without worrying that the victim is going to find out what is going on. All of this can come together to ensure that the manipulator can get what they want, and the victim often won't realize what is going on until it's too late.

CHAPTER 7: PERSUASION AND YOU

Persuasion: "the action or fact of persuading someone or of being persuaded to do or believe something." But what is *dark* persuasion, and how is it used? What techniques do the users of dark Psychology engage in when using dark psychology? In general, persuasion is an ambiguous term. I could *persuade* you to wash the dishes for me. A political candidate can *persuade* you to vote for them, based on a logical argument. Chances are, you were forced to write a persuasive essay or two back in high school English.

General persuasion involves the art of argument, presenting reasoning for why a certain action or belief system is right, important or true. Individuals who are good at persuading, like lawyers, can change the internal *beliefs* of a person and make them do a complete 180-degree flip.

Lawyers, politicians, police officers, negotiators, and religious leaders are all examples of powerful persuaders in an everyday context. There are more out there, and you're probably thinking of a few yourself. But dark persuaders are a whole different breed.

This is primarily because of intent. While regular persuasion usually contains no malice, a dark persuader has a darker motive. Positive persuasion, described above, is exactly that: positive. Usually, the persuader has a belief or set of beliefs that they themselves truly value and believe will benefit others if they are persuaded to their side.

Dark persuaders lack any sort of moral compass. The goal of persuasion is not necessary to change your mindset to something they value but to manipulate your way of thinking. Dark persuaders usually are acting in their self-interest and persuade their victims to act irrationally – at the expense of their own health or mental wellbeing.

Dark persuaders can also enlist the help of hypnotism to change the way you think about the motivations for your actions. While a dark persuader can influence you to steal, hurt someone, hurt yourself, and sever relationships, dark persuaders of capable of making you think you're acting intelligently and rationally the entire time.

SO WHO IS A DARK PERSUADER – AND WHAT DO THEY WANT?

So what types of people use dark persuasion, as opposed to hypnosis or brainwashing? Like most individuals who choose to use dark Psychology to manipulate others, these people have a tendency towards psychopathy or a lack of feeling or empathy towards other people. For a psychopath, the only needs and desires that exist are their own, and they have an insatiable desire to fill them.

Dark persuaders also use this technique not to just go after one person, but sometimes large groups of people. Think of advertisements for fast food, or a political speech usually full of lies and deceit (or at least partial lies and deceptive marketing). And yet, by appealing to pathos (feeling and emotion), most people are willing to believe.

This makes dark persuasion probably the most dangerous dark psychology technique in this book. It takes little skill, and if the manipulator is smart enough to gain a platform, whether it's television, books, music or even in-person speeches, they have the chance to persuade hundreds, if not thousands of people at a time. The same cannot be said for brainwashing, CEM, or hypnotism.

Dark persuaders are likely to be one of two kinds of people: your romantic partner, or a political/business figure with a popular following. Why? As always, proximity is helpful for the user of dark psychology, so a close relationship is always going to carry with it high degrees of success. Politicians and famous business people gravitate toward dark Psychology because of their large audience.

Take, for example, Donald Trump. When he won the presidency of the United State of America in 2016, many were stunned. But his appeals to populism and nationalism were right along the lines of dark psychology. Trump had already gathered a wide following from his business deals, casinos, hotels and television shows. He had the audience. Once he had a larger platform, the key was to repeat his main points over and over again.

The difference between dark persuaders and regular persuasion is the gap in logic between the two. For regular, innocent persuasion to work, there need to be logos or logic. For dark persuasion, users tend to rely more on pathos and sometimes ethos to ensnare their victims.

In one-on-one dark persuasion, the emphasis is still on pathos and ethos. A romantic partner might begin a sentence with,

"Well, if you really loved me you would…"

or

"I just thought that you cared a bit more about…"

See the commonality in the one-on-one persuasion? This usually involves a bit more guilt, as guilt tends to be a stronger, easier to wield a weapon at close range for manipulators.

THE LONG CON

The long con means exactly what you think it means when it comes to persuasion: This is when the persuader has massive amounts of patience (and desire to accomplish a successful persuasion). The persuader will draw out their persuasion if they have a tricky subject who catches on to them. The persuader can also use the long con if they are trying to persuade large groups of people (think of Donald Trump and his four-year presidency; now that's a long con).   Step one of the long con is trust and rapport. No matter how powerful a dark persuader may be, their work will be easier if they're met with less resistance. Those that they've convinced to trust them will likely put up less of a fight.

Then, once the chosen victim or victims have been prepared and are in the snare of the persuader, the dark persuader will strike.

Because victims haven't been brainwashed or hypnotized, they still retain some of their agency and ability to make choices. That's why dark persuaders penetrate every level of their conscious and subconscious self.

Once the trust and rapport are there, the persuader will start out with symbols and pictures, or "nonverbal signals." Unfortunately, this can get a bit dark, so just a warning:

It may sound absolutely nightmarish, but some dark persuaders do use their victims by convincing them to cause harm to themselves or others. If it's a romantic relationship or friendship, first, the persuader might bring the topics up in conversation. Then they might provide visual imaging, including movies, images and music videos with the intended theme. The persuader will throw their victim a bone every now and then – persuading them to make good (yet still bold) choices that benefit themselves, like buying a new car or adopting a new animal. That way the victim lets their guard down until the persuader is ready to pursue the rest of the long con.

This could take months, even years, but by then the persuader will have convinced that they and their victim have an inseparable bond. So even something so dark as murder is their ultimate goal, the persuader will have created the perfect coconspirator to help them all along the way.

LEADING QUESTIONS

Leading questions are a form of neuro-linguistic programming and persuasion that often benefit salespeople and politicians. Being verbally persuaded, especially face-to-face, is hard to ignore. If you've ever gone to a car dealership just to look around, and then found yourself driving a test vehicle off the lot, a salesman who knows the power of a few really good leading questions has probably persuaded you. Some salesmen may not realize that they are dark persuaders, while others train to receive financial gain. Politicians also train on their ability to use leading questions to persuade voters to come to their side and vote for them.

So what does a leading question look like? A dark persuader has a goal for what response they want from their subject, whether it's desire, guilt, pride, or something else. Often working up from creating a sense of desire is how dark persuaders use leading questions.

For example, a car salesman may say something like "So how fast do you think this thing can drive?" eliciting a response of interest and greed from their subject. Now that person does want to know how fast that vehicle drives. They'll follow up with "Now how does this car make you feel, compared to the one you're currently driving?" Sometimes a dark persuader will supply a few beginning answers if their subject is having a hard time. The salesman will respond, with a questioning tone in his voice: "Powerful? Sexy? Luxurious?" oftentimes the subject will latch on to one of these suggestions in agreement.

Politicians will often use leading questions masked as a rhetorical device in speeches they give to large groups. If it's campaign season, the politician might frame the leading question as a rhetorical one. "So do you think "this candidate" really cares about our country?" This interrogation suggests that there's only one answer: No. The politician may then follow up with "Doesn't that make you angry?" In which the audience, all subjects of this dark persuasion, really only have one option of response: "Yes."

Just like with any dark psychological technique, dark persuaders must be careful. Leading questions can be pretty obvious and visible, so a dark persuader needs to be gentle and patient so as to not give their subject an idea of what they are trying to do.

While we've all met the good car salesman, we've also probably experienced the discomfort and disgust of engaging with a bad salesman. Their techniques are obvious, and most likely you've been turned off because you can almost smell their desperation.

It is possible to regain control if a victim starts to sense that they're being lead down a path of thought and reasoning they don't want to be. If the dark persuader catches it by reading the victim's body language or verbal responses, they must stop and switch gears. If they try to proceed they're only set up to fail. They'll change the subject of the conversation, lull the subject into a false sense of security, and then begin to ask the leading questions again once they believe that they've come back out on top.

GRADUALITY

Graduality is very similar to the long con although the hints given to the victim to persuade them are a bit more obvious. Let's take a less malicious example. Remember the old Starbucks logo? Some might. It was brown, featured an entire mermaid with two tails, exposed breasts, and was encircled by the phrase "Coffee. Tea. Spices. Starbucks."

Gradually, over time, the logo became simpler and simpler and more minimalist as consumers became more familiar with it.

The consumers of the original Starbucks might have gone there once or twice a month, excluding the coffee fanatics that already exists. But over time, as the logo developed, Starbucks began offering more things. More styles of coffee. More snacks and food. More items for purchase. All the while, the brand grew and prices soared.

It's like the old folk tale of putting a frog in a pot of water and heating it until it boils. They won't notice it's too hot until it's too late. That's how a lot of companies with brand recognition function. By using graduality, they create a loyal customer base willing to spend more money than they would have ever spent before on a product like, say, coffee.

It's like building a staircase for the victim(s) one step at a time.

HIDING BEHIND THE MASK: TRUE INTENTIONS

The best persuaders have perfected their dark Psychology "poker face." This means, either when in contact with their victim(s) or not, they capable of completely hiding what their true intentions are.

For most people, this would be impossible. Almost everyone loves talking about himself or herself at one point or another. It's just another one of those dirty little selfish genes we all seem to share. It's easy to share your deepest desires, your likes, your dislikes and even your feelings. But it's even harder to not let on about what you truly feel at all.

How do dark persuaders do this? Of course, they *want something*, and they want it badly – or else they wouldn't be persuading you. Often they'll create a decoy desire to throw their victim off the scent.

The persuader won't shut down or try to avoid talking about what they want – they'll just come up with a really great, fake story to tell and have you hone in on, while they're doing their dirty work in the background. All the while, they'll appear like a normal, quite friendly and optimistic person, and no one will be every the wiser.

TRANSFERENCE

There is one last, very persuasive dark technique left in the dark Psychology user's arsenal, and that is the concept of State Transference. The persuader, whose aim is to hold all of the power in the relationship, can transfer their emotions, whether real or imagined, onto the victim whom they wish to persuade.

A dark persuader who has mastery of transference will use a specific recipe of verbal and nonverbal cues to transfer the desired emotions on to their victim. The persuader will first create a compartmentalized space in their psyche where the ideal emotion can live, while not interfering with their other thoughts, ideas, and reasoning.

CHAPTER 8: OVERCOME MANIPULATION

Once manipulation is identified, the next step is to get through it. Overcoming manipulation can be very challenging. In some cases, a 60 year-old-man might realize just now that his 85 year-old-mother is manipulative. They might never get through their issues, but they should still be confronted. Manipulation takes a part of both the abuser and the victim. It can ruin people's lives, altering the direction they take and affecting the rest of their years.

Manipulation can be hard to identify and even harder to overcome.

It can be done, and it should be attempted to get through. In a relationship based around manipulation, there might not be any coming back. Sometimes, people might just have to break up. You might have to get a divorce or stop calling your mom. It takes two people to partake in a manipulative scenario. Not both people will end up identifying it as a manipulative situation, however. In that case, the person that realizes what's actually going on might just have to move on, the manipulator never realizing the damage they caused.

This can be a challenging part of overcoming manipulation. Usually, some instances of codependency formed, making it even harder to break away.

KNOW YOUR WORTH

The first step in overcoming manipulation is for the victim to identify that they still have value. A manipulator likely took everything from their victim. They belittled them, ridiculed them, and made them feel as though what they thought didn't matter. In some situations, they might have even used gaslighting tactics to make their victims feel as though they're insane. It can be hard for a victim to then recognize just how much value they still have once they become aware of the manipulation.

Everyone needs to know, no matter who is reading this, that you have worth. Everyone has value. No one deserves to be manipulated. No one deserves to feel as though they don't have any purpose, reason, or value. You have the right to be treated justly, and with respect from other people. You are allowed to express your emotions, feelings, wants, and opinions. No one else has the right to tell you how to feel. You set your boundaries, and no one else gets to decide for you.

If you feel sad about something, that is completely valid. No one gets to decide if what they say hurts you or not. Not everyone might intentionally mean to hurt you, but that doesn't mean you're not allowed to still feel bad. You have the right to feel the way you do, and you have the same right to express those beliefs.

If you feel like you need to protect yourself, you are just in doing so. If you feel like your safety is being threatened, or someone is taking advantage of you, you have the right to remove yourself from that situation without guilt. No one gets to treat you badly, and though that can be hard for many of us to hear, it's the truth.

Manipulators aim to take these thoughts away. They want to deprive their victims of their rights to work towards getting what they want. This can't happen anymore. It's up to the manipulator's victims to now recognize their worth and stop the cycle of manipulation.

DON'T BE AFRAID TO KEEP YOUR DISTANCE

Many people that feel as though they're being manipulated end up being too afraid to do anything about it. They have been stripped of their own thoughts and opinions, their own feelings invalidated and instead focus on how other people feel. Those that have been continually manipulated might be afraid to leave those that have hurt them. They've depended on those that abused them for so long they don't know where else to go.

You're allowed to keep your distance. You don't have to feel guilty about protecting yourself. It can be hard to separate yourself from a manipulator, especially in a romantic relationship. You might see the very weaknesses that cause their manipulative behavior. Maybe in a relationship, a boyfriend's dad was an abusive alcoholic, and it greatly hurt him. It also caused his violent manipulative behavior that led him to hit his girlfriend on a few occasions. He indeed has his pain, but that doesn't mean he's allowed to inflict it on others. The girlfriend has every right to leave her boyfriend and find her own peace and protection.

Ask what is really lost by leaving the person that's manipulating you. More often than not, the value in a relationship is placed on codependent tendencies. A person is afraid to leave not because they love their manipulator, but because they are afraid to be alone. It can be scary to be on your own, but mostly because manipulators put that idea in their victims in the first place. Manipulators will trick their victims into staying with them because deep down, they know that the victim will be just fine without them.

IT'S NOT YOUR JOB TO CHANGE THEM

Once manipulation is recognized, the next step is to try to talk to the person about the manipulation. It's time to get down to the root issues of the relationship and figure out what can be done to help both partners get what they need, instead of just the manipulator. There has been an imbalance of power for far too long, and it's time to rebalance.

Unfortunately, not many manipulators are willing to admit their faults and later change their behavior. Instead, they'll do whatever they can to distract others from their faults, placing the blame on their victims instead. When this happens, the victim has to accept that their manipulator isn't going to change, and they must find the strength to leave.

There will likely be a desire to change the other person and help them improve their life as well. Not everyone will always be on the same page of their journey towards self-discovery. It can be hard to accept for some victims, but they have to realize that it's not their job to change their manipulator.

You can only help a person so much, and if they're not willing to change or improve themselves, it's not going to happen. Many people wait around for the other to change in their relationship, hoping their manipulation will get better. If a person isn't aware of their behavior and isn't actively trying to change it, nothing is going to happen in the end.

CHAPTER 9: PSYCHOLOGY OF MANIPULATION

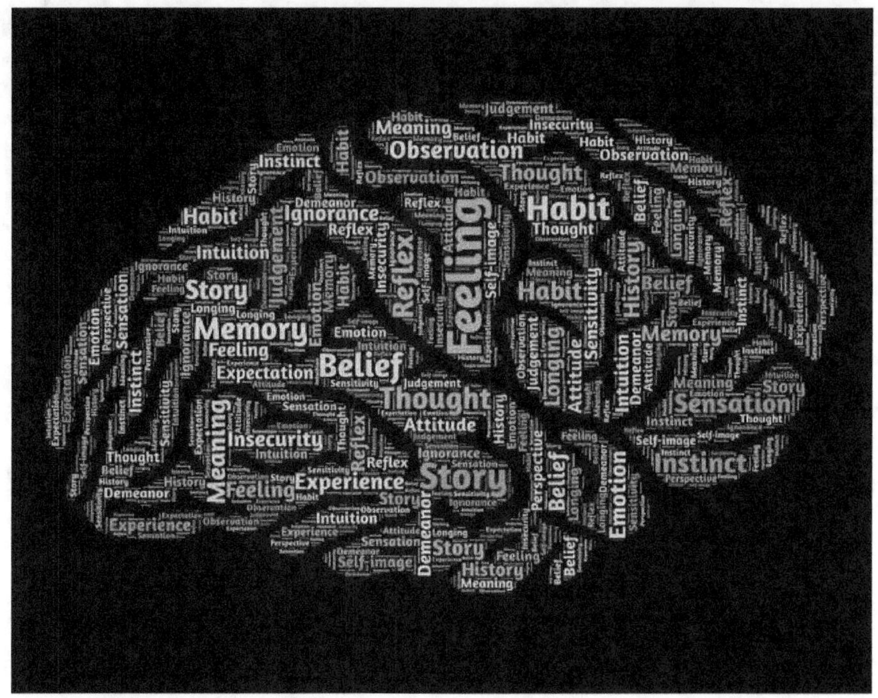

WHO CONTROLS OUR LIVES?

It's interesting to see that manipulation has been around for a long time, and that is not a new or imaginary concept. Understanding what the art of persuasion is all about is vital, to help you to deal with it.

In this chapter, we will look briefly at the psychology of manipulation. This allows us to see where it might occur in our lives. It will also help you in identifying those who might attempt to manipulate you. It is not only about people who like to dominate. If we don't know it is happening to us, it might be encouraged to act in ways that are incongruous to our normal personality and behavior. Learn how commerce can persuade customers into buying their goods and services. Recognizing such methods will help in dealing with the power of persuasion.

We like to believe that we are individuals who make sensible choices. In our personal journey of life, we do not always have full control, and we don't always realize this. As children, we are influenced by our parents and have little control over how we raised. Once in the education system, we are further manipulated. The teachers will tell us all about the social norms and what is expected of us in society. As adults, we are lured in by politicians trying to get their share of votes. Many are persuaded to vote for a party because of what they promise for the future, even if they don't necessarily believe in their policies. This gives such politicians power, and their decisions will affect our lives. Are we really in control of our lives, or are we merely influenced by those who know all the tricks of persuasion?

Later in this book, we will look at how to deal with various manipulative methods, even sometimes covert. First, you need to learn to recognize when you are being manipulated so you can counteract it. For this purpose, we will now look at what the experts say on how this sort of behavior can exist among us.

RECOGNIZING THE ART OF MANIPULATION

What then, in our everyday lives, do we need to be wary of?

Persuasive Language

The idiom that every picture tells a story, is very true. Words can be so much more powerful as they inspire and encourage us, even to the point of manipulation. How many times have you been inspired by a good orator, whose daring speech motives you into action? Words even influence when we are lost completely in a great book. The art of words can be so influential in coercing us to believe something, even when our eyes tell us differently. Communication is a powerful tool, especially when it comes to making people do things.

- Advertisers and salespeople use language to convince their goods are just what we are looking for. Using words, such as:

Affordable; Easy to use; Safe; Enjoyable; Time Saving; Guaranteed to last.

Note how all these words make us believe they are confident in their products.

- Politicians will use language, such as:

"We" - to encompass you in their world.

"Us" to make you feel a part of a team.

These are all communication tactics to make us feel included, so therefore important.

- Bullies use language along with aggressive behavior, to achieve their own selfish goals.

- Criminal predators, such as psychopaths, sociopaths, and narcissists, are all people who learn the use of persuasive language. This is a means to get their own way and gain control over another person.

SIX THEORIES ON PSYCHOLOGICAL MANIPULATION

1. Cognitive

There are many well recognized psychological processes in theories regarding the art of persuasion. One of those is the Cognitive Response model, developed by Anthony Greenwald in 1968. It is still relevant today for determining some factors in persuasion. It is also a model used extensively in the world of advertising.

Greenwald suggested that:

It is not the words of the message that determines the success of persuasion, but more the emotions of the *receiver*. The internal monologue of the one receiving the message will be deciding factor on how easy they are influenced. (2a)

Such internal thoughts will include positive and negative aspects, according to the individual's personality. This not a learning process, but more based on whether the person already views the message with favorable or unfavorable thought processes (cognition).

Overcoming any counter-arguments will rely on the expertise of the *persuader*. They should stop their target from having sufficient time to construct any counter-arguments. The *persuader* must encourage positive arguments to come to the forefront. This gives the "persuasion effect" a better chance of success.

Persuasion can be more difficult if the intended target has been forewarned. It allows the target time to build their counter-arguments if the "message" is counter-intuitive to their present cognitions. The importance of pre-warning can be seen in research conducted by Richard E. Petty, in 1977. The study showed that students given notice about a certain event were less likely to be persuaded that those who had no pre-warning. (2b)

2. Reciprocity

Another well-studied explanation for how we might be open to the power of persuasion is the Rule of Reciprocity. This is based on a principle related to social conventions. If someone does you a favor or does something good for you, then you are more likely to feel obliged to return the favor.

The Rule of Reciprocity can also happen subconsciously. Without even realizing it, you may agree to an action or favor asked of you by the requester. All because at some point they had done something for you, and you feel in their debt. You may feel obliged even if the request is something you would normally decline.

It is an effect widely used by companies who are looking to make sales. Often companies give out free samples or time-limited trials. This is not without a motive. It is in the hope that the customer feels obliged to return the favor, and buy the product or continue with the agreement.

Reciprocity is a recognized psychological process. It is an adaptive behavior that would have increased our chances of survival in the past. By helping others, it is likely that at some later point they will help you. Though, it can also have negative effects. If someone does something bad to you, then you may be driven by the rules of reciprocity to exact your revenge.

The Rule of Reciprocity is well supported by academic research. Burger et al (2009), suggested that a group of participants were more likely to agree to a request if the requester had previously done them a favor. (2c)

3. Information Manipulation

A powerful tool in the manipulator's armory. This is a method of being outright deceitful. It is a means of providing limited and confusing information to the victim. The effect of this will unbalance their way of thinking, making them vulnerable. It can also incorporate the use of intentional body language, to persuade and manipulate someone.

A study by McCornack et al. (1992) (2d) showed the different ways a message can be falsified to assist in the manipulation process. McCornack's theory has a premise of four maxims, in a truthful statement. A breach of any of these will render the message as intentionally deceitful. The four maxims are:

Quantity

This is the "amount" of information provided. Most of us seek to provide the right amount of information so that the receiver understands our message. Not too little, or too much, as that might confuse. A manipulator though would play with that quantity of information. They may omit certain pieces they consider irrelevant. Most especially if it is likely to work against their argument. This is known as "lying by omission."

Quality

This refers to the "accuracy" of the information provided. Truthful communication is one of High Quality. If we were to violate this maxim, then the receiver hears intentional mistruths. This is "outright lying," to gain the manipulator power.

Relation

Here, we talk about the "relevance" of the information to the message. To confuse or sidestep an awkward question, the manipulator may go out of topic. This is a way of changing the subject, for the sole purpose of misleading. It could be to hide their weaknesses. Or even to over-emphasize on something that will give them more power over their listener.

Manner

The "presentation" of the message. An important aspect of this is body language. We read inflections and facial expressions as we listen. A manipulator may exaggerate these to mislead the presentation of the message. This is all in the aim to emphasize their agenda.

Lying to manipulate or persuade someone is not a new concept. It is though, a method that is becoming particularly potent in the modern world. Online communication and social media do not always involve face-to-face contact. This makes it easier to tell mistruths or exaggerate information. A manipulator may in their elements with such communications.

4. Nudge

Not all manipulation is sinister. Sometimes we may be manipulated to help us make the right decisions for our good. To do this, the Nudge Theory is particularly useful. The Nudge Theory expands positive reinforcement, by using small nudges.

Skinner's studies or behaviorism, show how useful this theory can be. (2a) With positive reinforcement, such as rewards, it can manipulate people into behaving in the manner that you are hoping to encourage.

One example of "nudging" can be seen in this example. Adding exceptionally high priced items on a menu may seem counterproductive. Yet, the result of this actually increased the sales of the second highest-priced item. The customers were given a "nudge" in the right direction, but for the benefit of the restauranteur.

Richard Thaler, considered the father of the Nudge Theory, was awarded the Nobel Memorial Prize in Economic Sciences. (2f) His contribution to behavioral economics was considered quite momentous. Nudge Theory gives positive reinforcement, or as Thaler described it, it gives "nudges."

The Nudge Theory is not only effective in economics. It can be used to encourage behavioral changes and influencing personal choices. Even accepted social norms can be manipulated to changes, in this way.

Nudging is so successful, that in 2010, the British Government set up a Department Behavioral Insights Team. This was to help develop policies. The department was referred to as the Nudge Unit.

There can be obvious benefits of using "nudges" to influence people. It is still a form of psychological manipulation that can infringe on an individual's civil liberties.

5. Social Manipulation

This type of manipulation is also known as psychological manipulation. It is often a tool for politicians or other groups of powerful people who are used to advancing their interests. In its worst form, it is a means of social control. By taking away individuality, it coerces the populace into accepting what is given to them. Though it can have a positive side when used to help with personal issues, such as improving health and wellbeing.

Those in power who use social manipulation may use distractive techniques to deflect from important issues. They would argue that their proposals are for the benefit of the populace, and the benefit of your family and its future. Anything you think personally, that might be different, is wrong and selfish. This type of persuasion is very paternalistic, almost treating individuals as if they were all children. This "system" will strive to make the crowds believe the things that have gone wrong are, in fact, their fault. The only way to solve the problem is to listen to the guidance of those who know better.

Such a political strategy would bring to the forefront one social problem, only to hide another. It is a tactic to cause social unrest and panic among the populace. By creating unease in society, the populace will begin to demand changes. An example could be that the department wishes to hide the problems of health care. So, they decrease the budget in crime prevention, causing crime statistics to rocket. The populace will receive information to coerce them into believing the best way forward for the crime problem. The politicians will feed propaganda, by disseminating their *truths and facts*. It may not always be true, or it may be information that is exaggerated, such as misuse of statistics. This type of social manipulation could take years to get the end results that the manipulator requires.

The use of psychological manipulation is all a part of social influence. Professor Preston Ni, Communication Studies, published an article in Psychology Today. He indicates that *one party recognizes another's weaknesses. They deliberately set out to cause an imbalance of power. This enables them to exploit their victims, for their agenda.* (2g)

Does this make us all social puppets? To some degree, it does. Most of us comply and conform to what is expected of us to avoid a society of chaos.

Think for a moment, what is the latest gadget or home improvement product that you would like to buy? Is it something a friend told you about, or a neighbor owns? Chances are it is something that someone else has, or you've read that it's popular on the internet, and that makes you desire it. This is another side of social manipulation. We can be so easily swayed if we let our guard down. Whether that is a good or bad thing, depends on how you personally view it.

it can have positive aspects. The word "manipulation" might conjure up thoughts of a villainous individual/s bending you to their will. But, used correctly, social manipulation can help the populace, as a whole. Good examples of social manipulation are the "5 a day campaigns." Health specialists attempt to convince us to eat more fruit and vegetables. Or even the "stop smoking campaigns," which have resulted in reduced numbers of smokers. The result of which is a reduction in smoking-related diseases. This is coercion at its best.

6. Gaslighting

This is perhaps the cruelest form of manipulation. It is a means of casting into doubt on the sanity and self-esteem of a person. You could say it is *sowing the seeds of doubt* into the victim of manipulation. Working on a similar principle such as "knowing you are being told repeated lies." Until eventually you begin to believe the lies as the truth.

It is an unkind form of manipulation. The *gas-lighter* will cause their victims to lose all confidence in their credibility. This leads to destroying their self-worth. All because they begin to doubt themselves. That is the intention of *gaslighting,* to reduce the victim to a psychological mess. The manipulator will constantly put their target down by contradicting them. Also by convincing them that they are always wrong. Sometimes to the point that the victim will be accused of telling lies. This is why the victim loses all self-esteem. When that happens, they become ruled by the domineering influencer. It is a form of mental abuse, often seen in abusive personal relationships. The influencer will use constant techniques to make their victims doubt. Even to the point of doubting their memories, by denying things they've said and done.

Gaslighting takes a while before it is fully effective. The manipulator will wear his/her victim down over a long time. This type of manipulation is so insidious that it can eventually lead to the victim doubting their sanity.

Dr. George Simon PhD is a Clinical Psychologist at a Texas university. He has studied people with disturbing personalities. The results of his studies caused him to believe that certain types of personalities, particularly psychopaths, are very adept at manipulation. They will distort the truth and use aggressive language, to set the wheels of doubt in motion in their victim's thoughts. Eventually, the target will lose confidence in their judgment. They may feel shame and they will come to believe that the manipulator is right. This puts the target under the manipulator's control.

Gaslighting is not only restricted to individuals acting on one other. It can be argued that it also has political uses. Columnist and author Maureen Dowd is one to follow this belief. She argued that Clinton's administration used gaslighting techniques against a political opponent. Newt Gingrich, a member of the opposing political party, was often goaded into appearing hysterical. Some journalists and psychologists argue that Donald Trump also used gas-lighting techniques. Not only during his presidential campaign but also whilst in office. They argue he frequently says one thing, then denies he ever said it, which is classic gas-lighting.

CHAPTER 10: HOW TO MAKE FRIENDS AND INFLUENCE OTHERS

- Tuning

- Setting rapport with tuning

The ability to get along with people ensures success in almost any field of activity. If your work involves the need for joint discussion, team leadership, and other forms of mutual dependence, you certainly need to be able to communicate. However, this skill is necessary for everyone both in a narrow family circle and in a wide social sphere. The means or mechanism of interpersonal communication, ensuring its normal course and productivity, is given the name "rapport." A good rapport with another person creates suitable conditions for an effective exchange of thoughts and opinions. This is necessary for trade, after contracts, at interviews, consultations, and in all other forms of active development of relationships.

The ability to communicate is not limited to the content of our words and gestures. It implies a more complex and not always noticeable interaction. Sometimes, rapport is established as if by itself, and in these cases, we could call the formula for success a good "combination of characters": you simply instantly "find a common language" with a person. You can, however, come up against the opposite: a poor combination of characters. In these cases, you may want to stay away from this person, only this is not always possible, especially when it comes to relationships, in the family, or at work. In any case, with this approach, you risk missing out on a potentially meaningful relationship.

Using NLP, you can move on to a more mature and professional approach. Becoming a master of effective communication, you will gain more power over your relationship and the results achieved. You will still be able to enjoy natural rapport (for example, when communicating with an old friend), learn how to maintain and value such rapport without feeling the need to improve it. On the other hand, you will be able to use NLP techniques to set rapport in a wide variety of circumstances, especially in cases where it may not occur naturally.

Success often requires convincing others of the viability of their point of view: to influence, persuade, or influence to achieve change. Of course, any goals directly related to *communication* should satisfy the six principles of correctly formulating the result, which we talked about in the second lesson. However, other goals may also require the ability to communicate (perhaps to achieve intermediate results on the way to the final goal). Combined with the various result checks, effective rapport installation techniques will help you communicate better and achieve more.

Fine Tuning

Usually, we like those who are *like* ourselves. It's easier to get along with such people—that is, communicate more effectively. In turn, these people also like us — for the same reason. Thus, a good rapport implies conformity, tuning. Those who are in rapport tend *to behave similarly.*

Today we will tell you how to set rapport. You can begin to apply these simplest tuning techniques in just a few minutes. Other techniques require more developed skills and certain efforts to acquire them, which, however, are often paid off by subsequent practice: thousands of NLP adherents use these tuning techniques, making sure from personal experience that they are extremely useful for setting rapport.

To improve, you first need to learn how to determine when rapport occurs and when rapport disappears. This skill involves the development of "receptivity," sensitivity to what is happening to you and others. Such skills can serve as an example of what NLP calls *unconscious competency* as some use it with ease and perfection. The basis of normal communication is, among other things, those skills that, at first glance, seem innate. You can find examples of this in the areas of commerce, contracting, consulting, and other areas of interpersonal communication. At first, mastering these skills may seem like hard work requiring great concentration, but unconscious competence in any field (for example, the ability to drive a car) always comes with experience. To learn how to achieve sustainable rapport, you need to try to *do* it (in accordance with the four-stage success model described in the second lesson).

Understanding what happens when you install rapport will allow you *to choose the* most mobile and appropriate behavior. You will be able *to enter* into the communication of your own choice, and not just rely on unconscious skills. Learning to drive a car, you filter out the wrong skills and develop the right ones. The same thing happens when mastering communication skills. At times, it may seem to you that you are losing some skills and mastery, but overall results over a long period will show that you are really learning more effective techniques.

The ability to establish rapport benefits not only in the field of professional activity. It can have a beneficial effect on your goals, especially if they are related to communication. The secret lies in tuning. You can set a rapport, seeking an adjustment in several ways:

1. Physiology: posture and body movement

2. Voice: tone, the pace of speech, and other characteristics

3. Language and way of thinking: the dictionary used and the corresponding "presentation system" (vision, hearing, sensations)

4. Beliefs and values: what people believe in and what they consider important

5. Personal experience: the search for a common foundation in professional activities and interests

6. Breathing: a subtle, but very powerful means of adjustment

Setting a Rapport Using Tuning

Each adjustment method will be examined by us in turn and analyzed in sufficient detail so that you can begin to apply these techniques in everyday life. First, however, you need to understand some of the key tuning issues.

First of all, never forget how important it is to respect the tact and show respect for the interlocutor. Do not dramatically change the pose or intonation, as well as copy his gestures. Make any changes you need gradually and as inconspicuously as possible. Try not to draw the attention of the interlocutor to the language of your body movements, but do your best to ensure that he also subconsciously sets up a rapport. Otherwise, you risk annoying him, hitting him and even insulting him — and of course, then there is no question of any rapport. Although when establishing a rapport, you will first have to keep track of each of your actions—with time, they will become laid-back and completely natural. Moreover, your respect for the interlocutor as one of the many unique individuals should be sincere, especially in those cases, when his behavior and manners are different from yours.

Secondly, your respect for your own body should be just as sincere. We all stand and sit each in our way. Our other usual gestures are very different. This, in particular, means that in some cases, you will experience obvious inconvenience when trying to adjust, and the interlocutor will notice this. You may encounter circumstances in which deviation from the usual posture and gestures is already physically almost impossible.

When dealing with a stranger (for example, a new potential buyer), you can easily hide from him that your behavior is not typical for you in this case, but anyone who knows you well enough will certainly notice that you "left roles, "and this alone will destroy the rapport that you would be able to establish if you behaved as usual. Hence, try to stay in the "comfort zone," that is, within the natural boundaries of your personality. This does not mean that you will not be able to adapt to your interlocutor—just choose those behavioral features that will help you to adapt to your convenience or only partially.

Adjustment to Physiology

People who get along well with each other tend to take similar poses when communicating. Take a look at those absorbed in the conversation, and you will notice that their silhouettes often look like mirror reflections. After many years of marriage, older spouses often look alike.

The similarity is manifested not only in the general posture of the body but also in gestures and manners. For example, both interlocutors can sit back and clasped their hands behind their heads, or with their legs or arms crossed. Such imitation occurs quite naturally, and we hardly notice it. When rapport is established, our interests are focused on the interlocutor and the content of the conversation, and not on external signs. Such a physiological adjustment serves as evidence of rapport, which means that it can be measured, or *calibrated.*

The physiological adjustment can be used not only for measuring rapport, but also for its installation and subsequent fixing. To adjust to the interlocutor, you can:

- Sit or stand in the same position, change your posture or bow your head to one side;

- Cross or, on the contrary, free arms or legs; and

- Repeat his gestures with the movements of the hands, head, and body.

Partial Adjustment

Adjustment is carried out sequentially. You do not have to instantly start repeating the body language of the interlocutor in full detail. Start with one trait — say, a common posture or posture — then gradually adjust to the tilt of the head, cross your legs, reproduce the movements of the hands, the scope of gestures, the volume level and pitch of the voice, and so on. Tuning is a continuous process, not a one-time action. This means that by gaining experience and developing your skills, you can conduct experiments with partial fine-tuning at any level.

If the interlocutor has adopted a completely inimitable or too peculiar pose, then, for adjustment, you only need to *partially* change the position of the body instead of bringing this movement to the end. To set up and save a rapport, you don't have to imitate your interlocutor exactly.

For example, you may prefer a partial adjustment in the following circumstances:

- At the beginning of communication, to establish and measure rapport;

- In those cases, when fine-tuning takes you out of the "comfort zone" (see the example above);

- When the interlocutor is characterized by increased emotionality, which is reflected in the language of his body;

- In those cases, when the language of physiology is too unusual, and the interlocutor may notice that you imitate him;

- When a satisfactory rapport is already established, and you just need to save it; and

- At the first practical attempts at tuning.

What about facial expressions? If a person actively uses facial expressions — raises his eyebrows, rolls out or rolls his eyes, puffs his lips and so on — it is hardly easy for him to communicate with a passive, not betraying his feelings interlocutor, whose face is impenetrable, as if he is playing poker. People expect a similar reaction, and such an interlocutor, the response in the form of facial expressions will seem quite normal. You will soon find that such facial expressions are difficult to fake, so stay in your "comfort zone," that is, do not adjust to the facial expressions exactly, repeat it only partially.

When adjusting to overly noticeable posture features — for example, crossed legs or arms — some delay helps. You need to wait for some time and make adjustments so that these movements look completely natural.

You can use the option of partial adjustment — the so-called "cross-adjustment": if the interlocutor folds his hands on his chest, you cross your legs, and vice versa; if he twists his fingers, you can just put his palms together; if he rubs his hands, you shuffle with your foot, and when the interlocutor crumbles a plastic cup in his hand, click the pen button. As with partial tuning, in these cases, you are not trying to reproduce the actions of another person accurately.

Such actions most often require large-scale and small-scale physiological adjustment, adjustment at the macro and micro levels. Already in order to notice some of them, it may require great care.

Macro Fine Tuning

For fine-tuning, first of all, pay attention to your overall interlocutor's location with the interlocutor relative to each other and/or others. For example, if a person sits on the other side of the table or in a chair opposite, you can adjust to him as if you are looking in a mirror. On the other hand, you can sit next to him and look in the same direction, but at the same time adjust to his gestures and body position. In this case, most likely, you will be able to achieve a sense of unity and community, because you literally ended up with this person "on one side." However, at the same time, you are likely to experience difficulties when trying to establish eye contact, and indeed monitor the body language of the interlocutor.

In this case, you may prefer to position the chairs at a right angle: you and your interlocutor "look in the same direction" and at the same time you can maintain eye contact or simply look together in one document.

A "work" notebook or any kind of document that helps to focus attention helps to establish rapport. Such an object becomes a neutral reference point, common support for both interlocutors.

You will only strengthen the rapport if you start vying to make notes and edits in one notebook. At the same time, you will get the opportunity to adapt not only to the physiology of the interlocutor but also to his habit of drawing little characters or explanatory diagrams when communicating. Pass the pen to each other, mark something in the diagram one by one, or add an action plan to the items — this also helps to establish rapport. Such simple tricks can achieve real unanimity in thoughts because communication means the ability to get closer to a person not only in physical space.

The difference in heights also matters. Tuning is aimed at win-win rapport, not manipulation or domination. The difference in levels by elementary physical height (for example, standing and sitting) may turn out to be an incorrect signal, so this parameter must be taken into account when adjusting. If during the conversation your interlocutor walks back and forth, and you are spread out in a low chair at the other end of the room, it is unlikely that you will be able to establish a rapport. In this case, you should either join the mobile style of the interlocutor or achieve at least a partial adjustment — just get out of the chair. Take into account not only body language and gestures but also all the macro aspects of tuning.

Micro Fine Tuning

The depth of adjustment forms a continuous spectrum of particulars. The same applies to trim types. For example, with good *micro-tuning,* subtle physiological changes are taken into account. Although this adjustment requires keen observation, with its help, you can seamlessly achieve powerful rapport. By carefully observing a person, you will very soon begin to notice numerous individual characteristics, each of which can turn into an effective means of setting rapport. The interlocutor does not notice the characteristic signs of his own behavior, especially at the micro-level; in the same way, he will not notice your actions aimed at tuning — however, the rapport itself can be installed without any difficulties.

Some of these tricks may seem strange and even unnatural, but fine-tuning really helps to establish rapport. And what happens if the interlocutor notices your efforts to adapt to him? First of all, this happens very rarely. If this happened, then you most likely violated one of the described rules, left your "comfort zone" or forgot about the need to comply with all tact.

What if you have to communicate with someone who is also familiar with tuning techniques? This sometimes happens among businessmen and consultants. An interesting pattern is revealed here: most often, such an interlocutor will treat your professional communication skills with great respect. Ultimately, as we already know, the adjustment does not imply manipulation of the interlocutor, but the ability to better understand him and thus achieve a mutually beneficial result.

Adjustment to the Voice

Sometimes (for example, during a telephone conversation, when you do not see the interlocutor), the physiological adjustment will be impossible or inappropriate.

However, the pitch and tone of your voice also constitute an important parameter of communication. According to many studies, the voice itself often has a greater impact than spoken words. In any case, the more parameters you take into account when tuning, the more effective the rapport you set. This means that in essence, you need to try to understand the interlocutor and to adapt to him in all areas, in all respects.

The individual characteristics that you can identify in the interlocutor's voice include:

- *Volume* (How does he say loud or quiet?)

- *Tempo* (Fast or slow?)

- *Rhythm* (Can you catch a single melody in his words? Perhaps he utters them jerkily, in staccato rhythm?)

- *Height* (What voice does he have, high or low?)

- *Timbre* (What features does he have in his voice? Is he voiced or hoarse?)

- *Intonation* (What feelings does the interlocutor emphasize with his voice?)

- *Pronunciation* (Does the interlocutor use any characteristic words or dialectical expressions Considerations?)

As usual, start by adjusting to one characteristic, and then, as you gain experience, complement it with others. First of all, do not forget about the content of the conversation. Rapport is a bit like a dance. Make any changes as naturally and invisibly as possible. Remember that you should not be too distant from your comfort zone.

Do not try to imitate dialect pronunciation and peculiarities of diction — the interlocutor may think that you are mimicking him! On the other hand, try to adapt to the general level of conversation (as occurs when communicating with a child or person much older than you) and his style (in terms of formal logical clarity).

CHAPTER 11: SEDUCTION

Seduction can be defined in several ways, depending on which angle you view it from. It may be sexual, which is the most common definition. In this case, a person is tempted to engage in sexual intercourse. Often, such an individual may be opposed to this act. A less common definition is, ironically, one that is seen everywhere and every time. It involves enticing an individual or groups of people with any particular offer, which may not be as true as presented.

Seduction, both of the sexual and non-sexual kind, is used in marketing with increasing frequency. This is especially noticeable in recent times. Sparsely clad male and female models are used for advertising anything from undergarments to toothbrushes. Hence the common saying that 'sex sells.'

But this is not to hint that seduction is a modern concept. In fact, it dates many years in the past, even before Homo sapiens began to form societies. Seductive behaviors can be observed in various animals during their mating rituals. Don Juan is a popular fictional character, written as far back as the 1630s, who was infamous for womanizing. This would often involve seducing women of different types for his sexual gratification. To manipulate women into giving in to his advances, Don Juan might change his look. As such, he is depicted to be a shapeshifter; a cunning power associated with the devil. There is also the real-life story of Giacomo Casanova, whose unfettered licentiousness accounted, to some extent, for his infamy.

Femme fatale, as it relates to seduction, is a word used to describe a particularly driven seductress. In the English language, it is translated to mean Deadly Woman. These women are usually beautiful and self-aware. They use their sexual appeal and seductive charm as a weapon to bend the will of those they have targeted and, in so doing, achieve their goals. Other characteristics of the femme fatale are the blinding desire for survival, even to the detriment of their target of seduction. They may be selfish, cruel, single-minded, and determined. Some famous names, both in real life and fiction, in this category include Cleopatra, Lucrezia Borgia, Lilith, Lady Macbeth, Marie Antoinette of Austria, Morgan le Fay, and Salome.

The lack of empathy and manipulative devices utilized during seduction has been some of the reasons why seduction is associated with the dark triad, although these attributes are only observed in short-term seduction, as long-term would require more commitment.

TECHNIQUES OF SEDUCTION

There are a variety of ways but which a seducer may go about enticing anyone and getting them to act outside their will. The listed seduction techniques cut across both the sexual and nonsexual kind. They also include some popular methods of seduction and those that are more subtle.

Flattery: most people would detect this quickly and point it out to the seducer. But, if it is done subtly and the insecurities of the victim are taken into account, it just might go unnoticed. No one is without these insecurities. We all have, at least, one area in our lives where we feel inadequate and seek someone or something to validate us. Seducers who use flattery to get their way are quite observant and would prey on such weaknesses. They are often skilled at not being obvious, either with their choice of words or mannerisms. The reassurance they give to their victims is often very effective at gaining their trust. Sale marketers do not shy away from using flattery to convince their audience that a particular product is the best fit for them.

Mirror: in this case, the seducer tries to show to his or her victim they are similar, whether it is in their experiences, beliefs, abilities, etc. This works because of the notion of compatibility. We are often moved to choose those people, as relationship partners, business partners, friends, and so on, who share some things in common with us. When you see something of yourself in someone else, you would likely be drawn to that individual. The seducer may lie to their victim about their interest in a particular genre of music, simply to get them to feel safe and relaxed. It is even more effective when the shared experience is a negative one. The seducer might talk about how they have also been heartbroken by a cheating partner, just to get their victim to feel a false connection or bond. Where else do we see such in play? If you guessed advertisements, then you are correct. We are told that a brand is as family-minded or as fun-seeking as we are. As such, we make that product brand our personal choice.

Fantasy: we all have imaginations of what the perfect romantic partner would be. How they would behave towards us, the words they will say to us their sense of style, their goals, etc. The seducer, to execute their desire, may go out of their way to bring their victim's dreams and fantasies to life. They would get the needed information from studying their target or asking the person's close friends and family members. Then the seducer proceeds to become the victim's person of fantasy. They do the roses on the staircase, lights, music, and show interest in the victim's children if they have any, offer to fix certain things in the house, and so on. If done right, the victim, for that moment in time, feels like they have hit the jackpot. They are forthcoming with whatever is asked of them by the seducer. Some especially dark individuals may take this a bit further and derive some enjoyment from shattering the fantasy they had created. After all, it is all a game to them, and there were no actual emotions involved on their part.

Shaming: should the seducer not get their way, they might resort to guilt-tripping and shaming techniques. Unlike the method of flattery where the seducer enforces the ego of their victims and makes them feel good, shaming does the opposite. The inadequacies and faults of the victim are brought to light, and they are made to believe that their choices or decisions would only lead to unfortunate results, whether in the near or far future. This works quite effectively on people with low self-esteem. At that point, they may be willing to do anything just to please their seducer and feel worthy again.

Logical fallacy: these are errors committed during arguments whereby the reasoning of a person arguing is faulty. It may be done deliberately or unintentionally to misdirect, confuse, or make an argument seem more solid and whole than it actually is. It is done quite often by seducers, especially when they are being resisted. For example, a seducer might pose that their victims would yield to their advances if they, indeed, loved them. This is not exactly accurate, as many unrelated factors could account for why a person may refuse to give in to any request, sexual or not. The seducer could also argue that denying their desires at that particular point in time may result in a domino effect, which would ultimately cause the end of the relationship. This is called the slippery slope fallacy and is one of the most common types. These fallacious arguments are often delivered with such conviction of tone and mannerisms that it appears true and factual.

False control of decision: have you been accosted by a salesperson who, after some minutes of telling you all you stand to gain and lose depending on your decision, still says, in the end, that it is still your choice to make? In truth, it *is* your choice to make. This false sense of control makes the person being seduced feel like they are in charge, even as they give in to the request of their seducer.

Minimizing: this is another common tactic used by seducers in the convincing of their targets. They try to make a situation which holds great importance seem trivial. They would say things like, "this is not such a big deal" (this involves a fallacy called hasty generalization) and "everyone does this" in an attempt to make their victims believe there is nothing to be wary of. They might also go further to minimize the fears of the individual being seduced, by telling them to worry and that it does not betray the seriousness of the situation whatsoever.

Vilification: usually, when someone is trying to manipulate another into doing something against their personal choices, it is the seducer who seems like the bad guy. But, to get their way, the seducer might turn this around on their victim and make *them* feel like the villain for saying no. If the victim is a neurotic or one who is a people-pleaser, this tactic would work quite well in getting them to give in to their seducers. The seducer would pretend to be hurt and act the victim. This would place the actual victim in the position of the villain. A role I'm which neurotics and people-pleasers are uncomfortable in.

Pretending to be innocent: this seduction technique bears some similarities to playing the victim, but it differs in that the actual victim is not vilified and the seducer does not pretend to be hurt. Instead, the pretense is one of naivete, near cluelessness, and innocence. When it has to do with sex, they might tell their victims that they are virgins, and have only been keeping themselves for the right person. They make them appear unlike 'every other guy or girl' who only wants the victim for sex or some other type of material gain. The victim may also feel closer to their seducer if they are novices on the subject.

Seduction is a game that has been played throughout the ages, and one that continues to be a weapon in the arsenal of so many. The methods listed here are nothing new, but they expose the dark psychology at play during such manipulative activities.

CONCLUSION

Thank you for making it through to the end. There are many people out there with big goals and dreams of their own, who will let these go by the wayside because they are too worried about what others will think about them, about how this is going to go against the ethical and moral codes that they have, and about who is going to get hurt in the process.

If this all sounds like something that you would be worried about, then this guidebook was probably not a good choice for you to look through. We spent a lot of time taking a look at dark psychology and the different dark tactics you can use to get what you want out of life. From persuasion to manipulation to your special skills and characteristics as an empath, you will learn throughout this guidebook the exact steps that you need to take to use the different methods and techniques of dark psychology and get the results you need.

When you are ready to finally get what you want out of life, and you are tired of waiting for others to hand it to you, and you are tired of being nice and finding that life is passing you by with no benefits, promotions, or anything else that you need to reach your goals, then make sure to check out this guidebook and learn how to make dark psychology work for your needs!